David Mark spent more than fifteen years a
debut thriller became an international bests

He writes the popular McAvoy series, as we
and critically acclaimed psychological suspe
written for TV, the stage and is a frequent contributor to radio and
print journalism.

David achieved his goals while suffering from a catalogue of mental disorders.

He lives in Northumberland with his family and the voices in his head.

@davidmarkwriter www.davidmarkwriter.co.uk.

Also by David Mark

Darkness Falls
Dark Winter
Original Skin
Sorrow Bound
Taking Pity
A Bad Death
Dead Pretty
Fire of Lies (e-book only)
Cruel Mercy
Scorched Earth
Cold Bones
Past Life

The Zealot's Bones
The Burying Ground
A Rush of Blood
Borrowed Time
Suspicious Minds
Cages
The Guest House
Into The Woods

PIECE OF MIND

A Memoir of Folly, Melancholy and Madness

David Mark

© 2021

For my mam and dad, who do their best.

For my children, who don't need to.

For Nicola.

And for David Mark.

On balance, I'm glad you're not dead.

"Brave and honest and thoughtful" *S J Watson*

"A searingly honest dissection of an extraordinary mind - fascinating, heartbreaking, and very funny." *Roz Watkins*

"If you read nothing else, read this searingly honest book about the author's struggles with his mental health and addictions. It is unquestionably a book I'd want everyone to read to enhance their understanding of how adverse mental health can impact on one individual. I think this is a brave book. It is certainly a brutally honest one and yes, it's sometimes funny because only laughter will protect the raw and unvarnished truth. I really, really think everyone should read it." *Mary Picken*

"Absolutely loved this. Honest, brave, fearless, funny. Spot on about mental health issues and the perpetual struggle with existentialism that plagues all sensitive mortals. This book might just save a life." *Emma Haughton, author of The Dark.*

"It's the book that the mental health industry needs. A brutally honest and emotionally evocative read that moved me to tears." *Jenny Blackhurst, bestselling author of How I Lost You*

"A compellingly honest, brave, raw insight into what it's truly like to struggle with your mental health." *Claire Seeber*

"I have never encountered such an articulately and beautifully-written account of profound mental struggle as this. Many times I was laughing, crying and stunned at the same time. I never knew that was possible. As a trainer of psychotherapists, I need all my students to read this book." *Di Gammage, Child and Adult Psychotherapist, Play Therapist, author of 'Playful Awakening - Releasing the Gift of Play in Your Life'.*

'Darkly enlightening. Expertly details how it feels to be at war with yourself.' *Roger Lytollis, author of Panic as Man Burns Crumpets*

"For indeed who is not a fool, melancholy, mad?— Qui nil mo-
litur inepte, who is not brain-sick? Folly, melancholy, madness,
are but one disease, Delirium is a common name to all."

— *Robert Burton, The Anatomy of Melancholy, 1621*

"The thought of suicide is a great consolation: by
means of it one gets through many a dark night."

— *Neitzsche*

CONTENTS

PREFACE

For as long as I can remember, I've wanted to stop being alive. Not die, necessarily, but definitely cease to be. It seems the sensible thing to do, all things considered. Everything's dreadful, after all. And not-living has always struck me as substantially less terrifying than the alternative, which is to carry on existing and feeling like this, or worse, until the universe eventually relents and grants the sweet release of merciful oblivion.

I know, I know. That's a bit bleak for an opening line. But I'm trying to be honest with you. People have called me a liar a hurtful amount of times in my life so I've embraced absolute openness and truth instead. People don't seem to like that either. There's no pleasing some buggers.

So... suicide, eh? Feelings of overwhelming hopelessness and an unwavering conviction that it's better to jump out of the window than it is to die in the flames? Yeah, I hear ya. Up to you, of course, but I think you should give it a miss for now. I've heard it's not all it's cracked up to be. You might have thought about it so intensely that you've missed some of the less obvious pitfalls. Oblivion might well smell like the vegetable drawer in a student's fridge. Your life-force might not end up decorating the cosmos as a glittering speck of stardust and could instead become a breeze of bad air: a toxic waft of airborne unhappiness that drifts into somebody's head and tells them that they're dreadful. Hadn't thought of that, had you?

Or aliens might invade tomorrow and you'd be the silly bollocks who missed it. And don't discount the Buddhists. Reincarnation might be real. You could very well wake up in the consciousness of a pubic louse and have to spend your next life atoning for past transgression by becoming the most diligent and solicitous pubic louse you can be. You don't know, do you? Not really. You think it can't be any worse than this, but it really can. With your luck, you'll jump out of a window and some bugger will open a manhole cover just before you hit the ground. And the feeling does pass, if you wait long enough. It can't rain forever, can it? Give it another day and see how you feel.

No better? Still bleak? Bugger.

The thing is, you and I both know how a mental health memoir is supposed to go. I'm meant to have a few great years as a success in whatever field matters to me, then it all gets too much and I suffer from creative burnout and my brain suddenly pops as if somebody has stepped on a soufflé. Then I get better and overcome my demons and have a big cinematic celebration where I make amends for all that I've done wrong and go on to become something special and help other people benefit from my experience. You're meant to cheer for me at the end.

This memoir isn't that story and I'm not that guy. Sorry. I have the ugly kind of depression. There's nothing romantic about what goes on in my head. Sometimes I'm obnoxious and self-centered and I don't know whether that's my illness or me or a combination of the two. I don't even know whether there would be a 'me' if my illnesses were taken away. Which rather makes me wonder whether I might not just be a sentient disease. Cheerful, I know.

Anyway …

This little book is essentially a series of jottings, snippets, snapshots and scenes. In their entirety, they add up to fragments of a life. They're the closest thing I can give to an explanation. They might help you understand a little about living with extreme mental illness. If you already know all about it, these pages might help you feel less alone. It's a survival story, but the lead character is incredibly hard to like and you'll do damn well if you get to the end without wishing, on some level, that he would just stop moaning and get on with it. This doesn't make you a bad person.

In essence, it's about choosing not to die. It's about enduring. Keeping going. It's about fighting for your life when death seems so much bloody easier. None of us asked to be here, did we? And none of us are getting out alive. Why am I hanging about having panic attacks and breakdowns over electricity bills and failed relationships when I could literally switch myself off and be done with it?

Well, I've still got stuff to do, I suppose. And there's the kids, and true love, and the fact that despite being inordinately depressed, I quite like life and can't help thinking that at some point, everything's going to be unbelievably brilliant.

Confused yet? Sorry again. You've only got to read this stuff, I have to think it.

The thing is, I think about death every day. I'm a former crime journalist who now writes relatively successful murder mystery novels. I spend my every waking moment considering methods of execution, places of corpse disposal, and how to get away with murder. I'm a true crime enthusiast and I spend large amounts of time sitting in graveyards enjoying quiet communion with the dead.

I'm also a manic depressive. A Bi-polar Bear. I live in a state of perpetual wretchedness enlivened by brief spells of anxiety and self-destruction. I see things that aren't there. I hear voices. I vomit at random through the sheer weight of my own self-loathing. I'm an alcoholic, a serial adulterer and would willingly ingest poison if there was a good chance it would get me briefly high. I have Obsessive Compulsive Disorder and regularly enter hypomanic states of creative euphoria. I'm morbidly obese, bald, can't see a thing without my glasses and am working hard on my third bankruptcy.

Thankfully, I'm a magnificent lover, pretty cheerful and moderately funny. You genuinely won't see through the veneer unless I choose to remove it. And I'm choosing to remove it now.

This memoir offers up slices of my mind. It invites you to peek out through the eyes of a personality governed by illness. It looks at how it feels to keep fighting for your life when it's all too much to take and there's a chorus of demons whispering that you've done enough, taken as much as could be expected – that you're entitled to stop now; to walk to the pretty tree by the river, and finally rest.

I promise you, it's not a suicide note.

I'm better now, I think.

And I'll always keep going.

Even if it kills me.

1.

Little Grey Cell

I've always been unusual.

Odd.

Peculiar.

Eccentric.

An acquired taste. I don't know when it turned into an illness. When exactly does individuality become pathological? When does a personality become a disorder? When do our responses and our thoughts and our instincts stop being idiosyncrasy, and develop into a medical affliction? Am I my own silly fault? Or yours? Do I deserve your compassion when I act like an absolute twat? Does anybody?

I don't have answers to these questions, but I feel it important they be asked. And given my innate sense of self-importance and well-established delusions of grandeur, it seems important they be asked by me, a writer of mid-list crime novels and occasional dispenser of well-intentioned but uniformly bad advice.

Hi, by the way. I'm David Mark. So am I.

I talk about mental health, write about mental health, and have occasionally been referred to as 'expert' or 'advocate' by interviewers and reporters who've read it on my press materials and decided not to dispute it. I'm mentally ill, though I try not to let it get me down.

I'm absolutely bloody clueless about what's wrong with me, or with you, or anybody else. I don't know which bits of me are personality and which are the result of chemical imbalances and faulty wiring. I do know that at some point I realized that life was unbearable and I was the very worst thing within it. I was repulsive and loathsome, pointless and markedly unremarkable. I remember feeling quite confused by this new level of self-awareness, given that I was simultaneously steadfast in my belief that I was special, gifted, utterly marvelous and had, to date, been massively underappreciated within the claustrophobic halls of my tepid, beige world. I don't know whether I was made this way or evolved or picked it up like a verruca at the swimming pool. I don't whether misery is written into my DNA. I don't know very much about myself, and I've been having therapy for 25 years. So forgive me if I'm not brimming over with insights.

Anyway ...

I do know I'm a catastrophe of a human being. I've messed things up so often that it probably seems like I'm doing it on purpose. Maybe I am. Maybe I'm not. How the bloody hell should I know? I'm off my head. It's clear that things happen, or they don't, and fortunes rise, or they don't, and not of it makes the slightest bit of sense, even if you think about it every moment of every night and day until you puddle in on yourself like a melted pencil case.

Think on this...

We're mildly intelligent apes that live on a big spinning ball being orbited by a little white sphere that controls the tides. It's all highly unlikely, don't you think? I certainly do. I think a lot of things about life seem wildly improbable. If I think about them too deeply, my skin starts to prickle, and my head gets hot and my palms get sweaty and the next thing several hours have gone by and I realise I've written three or four chapters of a novel and I don't know what it's about, or I've driven 150 miles past my turn-off in second gear. My brain doesn't work. Or it works really well. I don't know. Can you see why the shrinks have stopped bringing a notebook to our sessions?

Oh, I used to be OCD, too. I managed to get a handle on all that when I realized that people were beginning to think I was a proper nutter. Overcoming the compulsion is the hardest fight of my life. If you suffer with it, by God you have my sympathy. It's not one of the cool ones, is it? OCD rarely comes across as enigmatic. It's hard to think lustful thoughts about the chap who's busy folding and unfolding his bus tickets with one foot on the step of the number 61.

I do know that I've always felt on the edge of things. There's always been a beckoning precipice nearby. I've always thought about death. I think about life, but that's all horribly fiddly and unwieldy. Death is simpler. Sweeter, even. Preferable, certainly. But for pity's sake, don't do it today. Things might be better tomorrow. And if they're not, well … something might turn up. You'd feel a right dickhead if aliens landed on a Wednesday and you'd offed yourself the day before.

I'm going to be completely straight with you about what the psychiatrists refer to as my 'suicidal ideation'. Suicide has always been lurking stage left. I have always been aware of my options. I've often been only a short walk or a swift swan-dive away from putting my troubles behind me. At certain points in life I've viewed it as the tempting dessert awaiting me at the end of a vile starter and a bland main-course. Sorry, if that sounds horribly matter-of-fact. I don't want to trigger anything in you. But if I'm truthful, and I do try to be, I've had one eye on the grave for as long as I can remember. Depression is a a charming, slippery and downright manipulative bastard. And I refuse to let her win.

Stick with me, won't you? I know this is hard work. But, well, you've probably read some Sylvia Plath poetry and dived into some misery memoirs, so you can get through this, I'm sure. Suffice to say, much of the path of my life has been mapped out by people's intentional brushes with death. The big things that have shaped me have all involved pills or heights or train-tracks. I'm still here though. I'm still holding on. And some days, it's no effort at all.

The shrinks like to think they can work it all out. Some of them have great insights and others have got me wrong so spectacularly that I've been left wondering whether I've been a part of some bizarre psychotherapy experiment. I'm a bit of this, bit of that, bit of the mother. I don't know what I believe and what I don't. I just keep keeping on. Maybe that's what it's all about, in the end. And on balance, I've made more good memories than bad ones.

Anyway, here I squat. Picture a toad loosely carpeted in packet ham. Stick glasses on it and a flat cap and something vaguely beard-like, and you'll get a passable approximation of the creature at the far end of your telescope. 43-years-old. Dad to many. A son, a brother, a father, an ex. A man in love. A believer. A mystic. An odd-bod. A celebrated novelist, once.   I'm on 225mg of Venlafaxine per day. 40mg of Rabeprazole for the chronic indigestion brought on by years of drinking a bottle of whisky a day and throwing it up in great orgiastic bouts of self-harm. Another pill, of late, for the high blood pressure. I don't care about that one so much. There's no symptoms.

The doctor seems to want me to take it more seriously but I've lived at least seventeen years longer than I ever expected to so find it really difficult to muster the appropriate levels of panic.

Depressive, first and foremost. No idea why. I'm clever, but nowhere near clever enough to find answers to the excruciating questions and accusations that my illness sears into the flesh of my brain each and every moment of each and every day.

So I'm collecting my writings, and scribbling down some more, and letting you wander about inside my head. You might be able to make sense of some of things going on in here. They might be of some comfort to you. You might look at my thoughts and impulses and be bloody grateful that you're you, or at least, not me. Or maybe you'll see a whiner. A weakling. A catastrophe of a human being trying to compensate for failures and shortcomings by waving a hand in the general direction of some vague, ethereal mental illness.

I'm gloriously Bi-polar. It was still manic depression when I first heard of it – a few months before Dad tried to end himself, and around the same time everything in my insides and outsides began to feel it was made of bile and bogweed. I'll get onto that, given time.

I hear voices. People talk to me.

I see things that aren't there. When I'm tired, everyday objects morph into horrific apparitions. Sometimes, I can't tell what's real and what's not.

I was a psychopath, for a little while, but I did the test again and it turned out I'd been answering from the perspective of a character I wear like armour. We'll get to that too.

Did You Hear The One about the Manic Depressive and the Borderline?

July, 2021

We're not short of letters after our names in our house. My partner, Nicola, has BPD and ADHD. She's absolutely Mad AF.

Has BPD? Hmm. It may be *is*.

She is BPD. Borderline Personality Disorder. And Attention Deficit Hyperactivity Disorder, which I used to think was the label that got put on children who stapled their scrotums to their desks or took a teacher hostage with a turd on a stick. Turns out it's a bit more than that. Who knew?

Nicola writes a blog about her conditions. She's very honest about her periods of depression and her mania and her suicidal ideation. And she won't mind me telling you this. She might mind tomorrow, but I'm somebody who thinks about killing themselves a lot so tomorrow can fuck the fuck off. Either way, I'm continually in awe of her emotional honesty. I know that if I had the same kind of loose wiring as she does, I'd be rocking back and forth in a rubber room and gibbering unhelpful things about the monsters in my shins. As it is, she's a professional artist, a mum-of-four, and long-suffering fiancée to an absolute nightmare.

As with my own condition, I struggle to determine where her illness begins and her personality stops. I'd like a traffic light system so I know whether I'm talking to somebody in a bit of a huff, or in the grip of a full-blown episode of acute mental anguish. Perhaps she and her mental passengers are twisted up in one another: wrapped around one another like fornicating snails. Maybe the illness squats, Gollum-like, in some dank, slime-patterned well of darkness deep inside her and only comes into the light when it needs to feed upon her energy and joie-de-vivre. Maybe it's a symbiotic relationship and pulling out the madness will leave the host body horribly reduced and enfeebled. I worry about such things a lot. I worry about everything. I call it 'thinking' but it's not. It's a feeling a lot like running downhill too fast: a desperate battle to stop oneself from crashing to earth in a chaos of tumbling limbs and darkness. I'm still on my feet, which is to be applauded, I think. But I know how close I am to the crash.

I'm at my desk again. Safest place really. Writing all this shit has stirred the pond in my subconscious and there's quite a lot of dead frogs and eel-scales floating to the surface and messing up my reality. Apparently I'm not dealing with the writing process very well and need to go back to therapy. Nicola is in therapy herself. She's got a good one and it seems to be going well. So well, in fact, that a few weeks back I felt as though the mood in the house was such that I might be in a safe enough place emotionally to embark upon a memoir about my mental health. This, it transpires, was not a wise decision.

We spent three excruciating hours yesterday performing some sort of avant-garde Scandinavian melodrama about a couple in escalating states of psychotic turmoil. The Guardian would have loved it. The setting was our bedroom. The players were she, me, and a spectacular caravanserai of emotional and mental baggage.

I started talking about some of the things that were causing me grief as a consequence of examining some of the worst moments of my life. I spoke about my guilt at the thought of this stupid and unnecessary exercise upsetting my mam. I spotted some of the inconsistencies and hypocrisies in my thinking and started trying to disentangle them out loud. I got cross. I always get cross. I do have a temper, I know that, though it's hugely better now I don't drink. It's entirely as result of frustration and almost entirely directed at myself. Why can't I work myself out? Why don't people understand me? Why can't I decide whether I'm cured or in crisis? Why won't anybody make it clear to me whether I'm absolutely marvelous or a big wobbling blobfish of utter shit and worthlessness

So I was ranting a bit. Stamping back and forth across the bedroom floor and aiming kicks at the air. It would probably be easier if I were more given to tears but I can never quite get past the notion that I look like a big girl's blouse when I start blubbing and always worry that Nicola won't be able to put her faith in somebody so given to sniveling. It turns to anger instead. Go me.

She froze on me, as she does. BPD stands for Borderline Personality Disorder. Most conditions are pretty horrible but BPD has to be the nastiest bastard in the whole pantheon of afflictions. You'll find yourself treated to a diagnosis of BPD if you experience at least five of the following things, and they've lasted for a long time or have a big impact on your daily life:

- You feel very worried about people abandoning you, and would do anything to stop that happening.
- You have very intense emotions that last from a few hours to a few days and can change quickly
- You don't have a strong sense of who you are, and it can change significantly depending on who you're with.
- You find it very hard to make and keep stable relationships.
- You feel empty a lot of the time.
- You act impulsively and do things that could harm you (such as binge eating, using drugs or driving dangerously).
- You often self-harm or have suicidal feelings.
- You have very intense feelings of anger, which are really difficult to control.
- When very stressed, you may also experience paranoia or dissociation.

Nicola ticks all the boxes. It's horrendous for her. Life is sometimes just too hard. People worried that getting together with somebody with all of my problems would be a recipe for disaster. Sometimes, they're right, though I'm at pains to point out that I've never been as emotionally healthy as I am these days, and she's definitely on a journey to a place where some sort of emotional stability might reside.

She's working through an unbelievable amount of her own shit at present. The day before our argument she had a session with her therapist that dealt with childhood trauma: abuse, neglect, abandonment. It took its toll. And a few hours later, here I was ranting and roaring and kicking up a stink about my own poxy feelings while she was trying not to come apart like a sugar sculpture in a rainstorm.

She started to cry, of course. And instantly every single part of my brain changed course. I wasn't angry any more. I wasn't even cross. All I felt was a huge great upsurge of compassion and guilt – a desperate wish for her pain to go away and to be able to rescind my raised voice and *Mein Fuhrer* display of anger. I've always been the same. Start crying and I swear to God I'll give you everything I own and swear fealty to your offspring if you just promise to feel better immediately. My mam's a crier, you see. Not so much now but when I was a kid I used to wonder if she simply had too much water in her body and that the tear duct was a release valve to make sure she didn't wet herself. Making Mam cry was the worst thing imaginable and somehow, I did it a lot. I'm genuinely in awe of anybody who can stay on course in an argument when the person they are at odds with starts to weep. It was a massive problem in my last relationship. I could never understand how she could press on with her venomous attacks when I was on my knees with tears running down my face. I couldn't understand how her anger could outweigh her compassion; how her need to make her point was more important than her purported love for me.

This, according to Nicola, is why I need therapy. I need to stop making everything about me. People have their own problems and sometimes I'm witness to them without being the cause of them and I need to feel strong enough in myself to let them work through it. Which is tremendous, on paper. The thing is, I've never felt strong enough in my relationships to let people be unhappy, however temporarily. I've always taken it upon myself to offer solutions, or support, or whatever the situation might call for, if it lifts their mood. Nicola believes this is because I hate the feeling of unpleasantness that pervades the home when one of the members of the family is in a state of emotional distress. So my need to be involved is actually selfish because the thing that matters most is removing the unpleasantness that is making me feel uncomfortable. Maybe she's right. She often is. The alternative is that I genuinely can't stand the thought of one of my loved ones being in pain and that I believe myself duty-bound to, and capable of, somehow making things better. I do, of course, make things worse. But the act of trying has to count, doesn't it? The trouble is, empathy was explained to me in a very unhelpful way. When trying to decide how to help somebody, I imagine myself in their position and try to work out what words or gestures or practical steps would make me feel better in that situation. And I act accordingly. This is depressing in two directions at once. Firstly, doing whatever it takes to help somebody feel better can make me feel even more worthless when the gestures fail to make a difference. And secondly,

I become painfully aware how rarely my own dark moods are met with any of the simple things that I know would make a difference.

I think I said that to Nicola yesterday, just before it all got unpleasant. She took it as an accusation that she wasn't what I needed. It was a criticism, and her BPD can take that feeling and turn it, quite quickly, into the suggestion that she either run away or kill herself. After five years together I'm hyper-alert to the signs of these changes in her mood but yesterday I was in such a state that I pressed on. I wish I'd shut up. And I said that to her this morning. She's emotionally exhausted. All of her defences are back in place and she's got a look on her face that would sour milk. She's hurt and exhausted and doesn't want me anywhere near her. If I were emotionally robust I would respect her wishes, but I'm not, because I can't imagine anybody being left alone to work through their problems coming to the conclusion that they should come and find me and accept/offer a hug. The conclusion, if left alone, will be to leave me. Why the Hell wouldn't it be? I did this, with my temper. I did this, by dumping my problems at her feet while she was still processing her own. I've enabled her, you see. All those times she's been too emotionally wrung out, too depressed, too angry, too; suicidal to even function, I've been enabling her to stay in that headspace. I don't actually know what I should have done differently but she and her therapist aren't really fans of my approach and hope that, now she's getting better, I'll offer my 'support' in a different way.

My trouble is that I have a massive inability to shut up. But apparently, shutting up means stuffing my feeling back down deep inside and ramming the lid on, and that's not great either. So really, I need a therapist who I can shout at until I feel better, allowing me to spend the rest of my time being supportive in the right way. I've enquired whether or not I might also be permitted a bag of words and sentences that have been pre-approved so that I don't actually cause offence by saying something triggering.

The truth of it is that Nicola is a vastly more impressive person than I am. She's better looking, more talented, more insightful and the recipient of more unconditional love from her partner and children than I could ever dream of. I think I'm probably jealous, while being massively proud. But I get frustrated with how brittle her spirit seems to be and how little she acknowledges her own awesomeness.

And then I remind myself she has BPD and ADHD and a history of suicidal ideation and that she comes from a background that is almost Dickensian in terms of emotional nourishment. And I instantly feel like a proper arsehole for doing anything whatsoever that isn't nurturing or rewarding or entirely aimed at making her feel good and loved and valued. So I decide to go find her and tell her she's marvelous. Sometimes, in these situations, she's already put herself right and we hug and cry and move forward. But she suffers from an emotional hangover from such explosions and invariably feels too wrung out and exhausted to do anything, which means I then take on more responsibilities and she feels more guilty for not being able to contribute the way that she thinks she should.

I don't know whether today is such a day. I wish I was strong enough to just leave her be and trust in her love for me. But I don't trust in her love for me, because I don't feel even slightly deserving of it. And I know she could make me feel better about that by saying this, or that, or any one of the things I say to her and which she dismisses as platitudes. And it doesn't matter that she tells me she loves me five or six times a day. It's the things she doesn't say, because she isn't the kind of person to say them, which leaves me desperate and vulnerable: a baby chick squawking to be filled up by something, anything, that will plug the yawning hole inside me.

So yeah. I'll probably ring the therapy place and get booked in. I don't know if it matters whether it's for me or for her. I'll do the work. I'll try and get well so I can be strong enough to back off, as counter-intuitive as that might seem. She's right. I shouldn't use her as my therapist. She's my fiancée and the mother of my child and she's unpicking years of abuse with some seriously intense therapy. Which makes me feel like a selfish prick, now I think about it. Typical of me, actually. Typical of the way this pathetic, snivelling little bastard has always acted: selfishness and self-pity masquerading as benevolence and generosity of spirit. No wonder she can't tell me the things I want to here. Who could love this?

Best think of something funny to say. Best think of something poetic or erotic or earnest that might serve as a chisel to chip away at the ice wall between us. A laugh is unequivocal, isn't it? If I get her laughing, she'll like me again. If I turn her on, she'll be drawn to me.

If I send her some prose she'll see my beautiful heart and remember that I'm a decent writer who might get back to the bestseller list some day and is probably a decent bet long-term. And then I consider my own desperation and the way she sees through it and skewers my true nature to the wall like a lepidopterist pinning a wriggling shit-brown moth. And I decide to stay in my office and feel miserable until my guts are churning and I need to go and vomit out all the filth and repugnance and bile. I'd like to think that if she hears me puking until my eyes pop, she'll remember that she loves me and come make things better. And if she doesn't, it's because I'm a worm who doesn't deserve it. There's no third option. I'm David Fucking Mark. I'm a clever bastard and if I haven't thought of something then that something doesn't exist. Which does, apparently, come across as arrogance, which is ugly, as opposed to self-confidence, which somebody once told me was sexy and which I dutifully assimilated into my day-to-day persona 25 years ago.

So I'll sit and write, and I'll read it back and make changes, until it's pretty but less true. And I'll maybe email her it in a state of absolute blackness of spirit in the desperate hope that it will make her feel something towards me that comes close to love. Then, yeah, I'll phone the therapist. The only way is up.

She just came in and hugged me. She's so spectacularly beautiful that I want to cry. But I don't. I can't. So I make a joke and tell her she can read this, if she feels up to it.

I'm so much better written down.

3

Seeing things, and Not Seeing Things

"There, look. Dave, can you see it? Look, quick, look!"

I'm looking. I'm staring so hard at the sticks of dry bracken and sun-toasted ferns that I fear setting them alight. But I can't see the little grass-snake. Uncle P can see it. He's got thick glasses that go dark in the sunshine and they help him see hawks and lambs and fell-ponies that are nothing but a smudge to me. I haven't got glasses yet. I'm still squinting at stuff, the way he does whenever he takes his off and goes all mole-ish. He's unbelievably pleased with our find. Energised, like we've scored a goal. He's looking at me all pleased and gormless and saying we've got lucky, proper struck lucky. It's as if a unicorn has just pranced across the field, or the car from Knight Rider has leapt over us: a quick salute from Hasslehoff as he glances down and spots us here, squatting low, tucked in by the footbridge, at this quiet little glade by the river.

So I agree.

Yes, it is. It's amazing.

And yeah, of course I saw it. I saw the snake.

I'm seven or eight, I think. 1985, or thereabouts. Still supporting Liverpool, because my best friend supports Liverpool, so it seems like the right thing to do. I'm into my football. I'm a natural number 11, the tricky winger who might bag seven or eight goals a season from the flanks. Love Steve Nicol and Ian Rush and the Australian with the poodle haircut, though Dad says they might not be the same without King Kenny. Uncle P doesn't know about football. He knows about computers and cars and Chris Rea. He's a fussier eater than I am. Beans, turkey drumsticks, Jaffa Cakes, toasted teacakes. He's a good adult to point to when Mam's tearing her hair out over the pathetic amount of foods I'm willing to consume. P doesn't eat vegetables, and he still climbs mountains and walks miles. And Mam eats salad and healthy stuff and is always poorly. P eats what he likes. He's demonstrably happy, is P. Doesn't seem like he worries much. Doesn't shout. Always has a new car with a proper new-car smell. His phone number is only one digit different from ours, and that's proper weird apparently. He's into his music. Plays bass guitar and owns a computer with an actual flight simulation game. He would like to learn to fly, some day. He took me in the cockpit of the big Hercules fighter jet out at Carlisle Airport once. He'll get his chance when he comes into some money not long from now. Won't get his licence but he'll master the basics. He'll suffer from depression too.

Mungrisedale today... Mungrisedale most Sundays... Big flat valley drifting up towards chunky, green-brown fells. Gorse bushes too spiky to allow football so if we do anything sporty today it will be rounders, with Mam's Mam trying not to wet herself as she laughs on second base, and me getting cross because nobody's playing properly. Eldest grandchild. The other two are too young to realise this all matters.

P and me usually go off for a stroll. Dad goes off for one too, though he drifts off in another direction. Needs time to himself. Needs the space to let his brain have a rest. Likes to saunter off and find new things and give his mind an airing. P and me usually head to the rock: huge great whaleback of sparkling stone, over the river and past the yellow-speckled bushes. Sometimes we pull up ferns and use them as spears: mud-caked tips slapping down onto long, tangled grass.

We've come the other way today, up and past the curve. Out of sight. The river crosses the road here, a few inches deep. I argued with somebody about whether it was a fjord or a ford, and P said he wasn't sure but if we had a party here it would be a Fjord Fiesta, and then he laughed, so I laughed.

He's talked a bit, in that way of his. Joking, but sincere underneath it. Fell-boots, fell-socks, trousers with lots of zips. He might have his camera with him. Might be wearing a baseball cap. Still got the beard that the cancer will take when I'm coming up 13.

So we're down in the grass, talking snakes. We talk about all sorts on our walks. There's lots to talk about when football's off the agenda. Tortures, usually. P knows loads about loads. Thumbscrews, flails, iron maidens. Told me one summer about the African tribe that smears a chap in honey then imprisons an angry rat beneath a coconut shell on his chest. It goes mad for the honey and picks the shortest route to it. I can picture it. I can picture it the same way I can remember scenes from movies or pages of books. He likes being my naughty uncle. Likes that I think he's cool.

Snakes, now. Talking about snakes. We have adders, apparently. They can kill you, if you're a bit fragile to begin with. He's seen a couple over the years. Loves the countryside, does Uncle P. Can point at a lump of horizon and tell you the name of the fell, how tall it is, and which is the best way to climb it. Makes them up if he isn't sure. Got me in trouble when I told Mam we were climbing Donkey's Dick.

"There was a Viking chief who was killed by being thrown into a pit of adders. That's quite the way to go. If that's how I die I know it will be something for them to talk about at work…,"

We get onto serious stuff by accident. He asks if I'm still hearing weird sounds. He's asking about the creepy whoosh-whoosh-whoosh noise of catarrh in my ears but I don't realise that's what he means so I just come out and say it all matter-of-fact, like it's normal, like it's what everybody has going on inside their heads.

"It's more a feeling than a person. A funny language. It's so weird. I can feel it as much as anything. Just there, above my ear. Just somebody talking away, chattering to themselves. I don't think they even know I'm there."

He looks like his sister for a moment: that expression that says I'm telling a tall tale or exaggerating or being over-dramatic. So we leave it. Talk about Dad instead. He's a good dad. Loves you so much, don't ever forget it. Got such a good brain in that head of his and life can be hard sometimes. It was nice to see him tucking in during the picnic, wasn't it?

And then we're back down on our knees, nettling ourselves, scrabbling through the ferns, and P 's swearing to god that he saw a baby grass-snake – a little 'S' of flickering emerald. I don't see it. I draw it in my workbook at school the next day and I tell everybody that I saw the grass-snake, like P did, but I never saw a thing.

I see it now, though. All these years later I can see that grass-snake as bright as if it were freshly painted. I can see the river and the sky and the shapes of the clouds. All more invention than memory, but no less real for that. I can see Dad too, coming back from his walk. My little brother had gone with him, as it goes. Kept Dad company while he was alone.

Mam asked, not long after. Asked the same question about whether I still heard weird stuff. I told her about the whoosh-whoosh-whoosh and we got back in to see the specialist. I think there was another operation.

There wasn't a specific moment when the voice started speaking in a language I could understand. I just picked up bits and pieces and at some point we became fluent in one another. He didn't have very nice things to say. None of them did.

I've been back to the same spot countless times. Fell down the rock when I was still a kid. Put a lumpy bruise right on my spine. I said my cousin pushed me but I don't know if he did. I think I just fell, and he was there, and it made for a better story. I can see both versions as clearly as one another and neither is filed in a drawer marked 'truth'.

We stop at Caldbeck on the drive back. My auntie gets an ice cream. We don't. My brother's lactose intolerant, which means I have to be as well. No money, either. And it's too risky to eat sticky stuff in somebody else's car.

Good day, all in all. Home inside the hour. Grandad drops us off and I'm up the street in moments, off to tell my friend about the grass-snake. He's well impressed. Likes the details about the teeth.

Dad knew I hadn't seen it. I don't know how, but he could tell. He sometimes saw things on his walks too.

Didn't spoil it for me though.

Didn't say a word.

4

DNR My DNA

From my Dad I got my…

- Scorn
- Cleverness
- Silliness
- Tolerance
- Intolerance
- Temper
- Unbearable sadness
- Fortitude
- Insight
- Fight
- Sacrifice

From my Mam I got my

- Worry
- Music
- Certainty
- Standards
- Nervousness
- Hyper-vigilance
- Mistrust
- Exasperation
- Disguise
- Pretence

The rest is just me.

5.

Living With It

Headache in my shoulder again. Steel pincers at the top of my spine. Toothache at the base of my skull. The smell of blood and old keys and chopped liver.

Always the same place. Always the same pain.

Bulging eyes, sometimes: the feeling of thumbs against my eyelids, pushing out, not in.

Same pain that punched me insensible at eight-years-old. I'm no stronger now. Better at dissembling, but no higher tolerance for the agony or the emptiness or the starbursts against the black.

Same feeling of having been built of plasticine then condensed with a flat palm.

Shorter than I should be. Denser. Squat and lumpen, with my stocky legs and broad back and big round aching head.

I rub my palms across my temples, kneading the lumps, knuckling the knots and gristle. The pad of an index finger against my sinuses; perhaps a crooked thumb-joint between my eyes. The pain lifts like dust, settling back as I look away.

Don't slouch, David. Don't grind your teeth. You hold your jaw too tight. There's so much tension in your tendons, your muscles, your joints, your bones. Dislocated jaw doesn't help. A crunch like biting ice: the hinge beneath my ear popping in and out; the gunshot 'clunk' less satisfying than it sounds.

Aching for somebody else's hands. Aching for expert tenderness: meaningful manipulations of the places I can't reach.

I blamed addiction for a long time. The headaches were hangovers. Self inflicted. Own bloody fault. Drink more water, you prick. Sleep less crumpled up. Eat a real breakfast and try a vitamin or two.

Sober now and still it feels like my bones are crumbling. Pain in my face, my brow, the top of my head, down the elevens at the base of my head, splitting in two to grind, grind at my shoulder-blades.

He suffers from headaches, said Mam, years back. We think he might need glasses.

And I'm sitting there beside her, trying not to let it be anything too serious. I don't want him shining his torch in my ear again. He'll see them in there. In here. In me. Muscled limbs and gargoyle faces, leers and howls and red-black fire. They'll see him too. Pull him in, maybe. They're calling him names. Calling me names too. Protests at the lack of space. Rhythms beaten out with shin-bone sticks: syncopation on the malleus, the incus, the stapes. There are knees and elbows and heels pushing up against bone and brain. They kick through the membrane of my ear drum and make me blame it on a cotton bud…

Your head hurts because you're weak, David. Same as the ear infections. Same as the problems with your adenoids. Same as why you're always in a headlock, or getting dead legs, or having to walk home three miles out of your way so nobody asks you questions or kicks your legs out or takes your watch. That's why you're not in the football team. Weak. Small, and fragile, and pathetic.

Mam there, next to me. Dark haired. Small framed. Fragile.

Neurotic, says Dad. Pathetic, when she cries.

Lovely person, says Nana.

Heart of gold, says Auntie S.

I get glasses. They help, for a bit. Do their job, if nothing else. Keep the pollen out of my eyes too. No PE for David, he's allergic to the grass. Allergic to the sunshine. Allergic to rough play. Stay inside, read a book, disappear inside the pictures in your brain. The voices will make room.

Safe here. 43, and inside on a warm day. Headache in my shoulder, an ache along my jaw. Unprotestingly prisoner in this room full of books. Feeble. Weak. Small.

Something that isn't quite prayer – hovering at the horizon of my thoughts. A plea for elongation; for the stretching of my spine – for restitution of stolen inches; an Almighty intervention, mercy overdue.

Drink more water. Just drink more water.

It shouldn't be that simple. Shouldn't be something so damnably bland as cause and effect, of action and inaction and inevitable consequence. It has to be a pain born in the cerebral cortex. Has to be punishment for sin. Has to be an agony earned through immorality and agonized contemplation.

I'm sorry. Shouldn't that be enough? Shouldn't sorrow be payment? Make it stop. Make it hurt less. Please.

I can see myself in the toilet cubicles now, screaming into the acid-splashed bowl, one knuckle pressed hard into the muscles at my neck, grinding on the pain until the last of my stomach lining shoots up in a bitter tide of whisky and bile.

You deserve this.

Do it again.

Do it again.

I won't drink. I won't slide back onto those grimy tiles; head against the cool porcelain; dizziness thudding inside my skull. I'm better now. Better than ever.

Headache in my shoulder.

Rope burn of tightening pain, hot beneath my jaw.

5.

Supermanic Black Hole

I've always had a hard time accepting that I experience the opposite of depression as part of my illness. I don't see myself as somebody who gets over-excited or particularly hyper. I have a very clear picture of what mania looks like and I don't really see how it has anything to do with me.

Those who know me best have a tendency to laugh in my face whenever I suggest that I don't experience the highs which counter-act the lows. So do the mental health professionals. They suggest, as politely as they feel necessary, that most of the relentless fuckuppery of my adulthood has been a consequence of my excitable, deluded, and inceasingly unstable mind. But you can take what most of those buggers say with a pinch of salt. I once paid good money to see a psychotherapist who had a Live, Laugh, Love poster on her waiting room door, so don't go thinking they're any more clued in than the rest of us.

Anyway, it turns out that mania can present in numerous different forms. In my case, it's a sense of grandiosity. Of unparalleled potential. It's a conviction that all will be absolutely marvelous and that we don't need to worry about a thing because I'm David Fucking Mark, the chosen one, and I understand the universe and know that I'm special and that anybody who disagrees with me is absolutely trying to suck the positive energy out of the room with a big old hoover because they don't like to see me happy.

So, yeah, maybe there's a kind of giddiness about me that bubbles up from time to time. But manic?

Perhaps it's the tall tales I used to tell when I was little. I'd really struggle with truth. Telling people what actually happened always fell so far short of how amazing it would have been if something else had happened instead, so I'd tell the story my way and end up in trouble with all and sundry for telling the neighbours that my brother was dead, or informing my teachers that a firework had exploded in my dad's face, or that I'd seen the lad who bullied me busy drawing glasses and a beard on an old portrait in the school library and that he'd threatened me with a knife when I tried to stop him. All bollocks. All made up. But never dull. I always got a reaction and could never understand why people were so cross with me afterwards.

And yes, it did carry on into my teenage years, when telling lies were so much easier than telling the truth. If you're somebody who can tell their mum that they won't be home until late because your girlfriend's parents are away and she's decided tonight's the night she's going to let you touch her nipple, then God bless you, you're a strong character and your parents are ace. My mam used to act like I'd get somebody pregnant if I looked at them without condoms on my eyes, so fabrication felt forced upon me. If people are going to say 'no' in answer to a request for permission, isn't it simply common sense to word the question differently? "Can I go to Andy's and watch a movie?" is so much more likely to yield a 'yes' than "Can I go to my girlfriend's and growl into her cleavage until I'm dizzy?"

Manic? Don't be daft.

And yes, I suppose I did quit my job on a whim, and then I spent all the money I got from my big book deal on holidays and clearing other people's credit card bills, and I've drunk to such excess that parts of me don't work any more and I have little memory of my thirties, but that's just alcoholism and a desire to impress, which is a long way short of mania, isn't it?

Having another baby? No, we were caught up in the moment, happy with ourselves, feeling good. You're not going to spoil that for me. You're not going to say we had Artemisia because of a flare up with my mental illnesses. That's so mean.

No, this is who I am. I do stupid things and say stupid things and feel absolutely dreadful afterwards. I book holidays we can't afford and make promises I can't keep and I try desperately to make the reality live up to the fantasy and when I fail I fall into a depression that only unnatural giddiness and glee can pull me out of.

But manic?

6.

A Conversation Between My Selves

So, yeah. I'm writing this thing. It's not like my usual stuff. It's... well, I don't know, really. It's about me, and you, but ...

Ha! Favourite subject, then.

Yeah, ok. But no, that's not it. It's like a memoir, but about what it's like living inside this head. About fighting the demons, as it were. Fighting you, really, though I don't want you thinking you come out as the bad guy. I'm a nightmare, I know.

I don't like the sound of this. You've got all excited before and it ended up going horribly wrong. What is it that makes you think you have any business writing something like this? There are people with real problems out there. People who've really suffered. Abuse. Neglect. You had a nice family and loving parents and you've had every opportunity. Don't start blaming me for where it's all gone wrong. I'm the only one who's ever there for you.

I know that. But, well ... the hearing voices. Seeing things. Making mistakes and not knowing whether they're a result of my mental health problems or if it's the other way around. Y'know, a look at where madness begins and personality stops. Like, could I have been different? Would I want to be? It's all quite nebulous as things stand. But, I've always been on the edge, haven't I? Always had a bit of a preoccupation with stepping out into the void. And the sadness, when it comes – the rage, the venom, inertia of trying to do things right and not get things wrong and ending up static and sobbing and curled up like a morbidly obese fetus ...

Run out of ideas, have you?

No, I have endless ideas. I just feel like there might be some kind of interest in it. I mean, not me as a person, but just, my relationship with the dark stuff – living with it all, and not living with it. All the slippery eels in the family gene pool . Being around suicide. Living with somebody whose demons play rough. Just about madness and me, and ...

Oh my God, your self-infatuation is simply epic in scale, isn't it? You actually believe there's a market for your thoughts? What next? Will you be freezing your tears and selling them as lozenges to people who need an injection of oh-so-earnest sincerity…

Don't be like that. Please, it's hard enough starting this without you making it worse …

You're not famous, David. Nobody wants an autobiography from somebody they haven't heard of.

It's not an autobiography. It's just thoughts and stuff. I mean, I've been through things …

No you haven't. Not compared to people who've really suffered. You weren't battered or neglected. You weren't even sexually abused!

Well, Nicola says that I might have been, actually, if I change my perspective on some stuff. She says that half my problems are to do with sex, and not feeling worthy, and compensating for deficiencies of character and height ….

Nicola is in no position to tell you anything. She's more insane than you are. And she chose you, which means she's entirely devoid of discernment. You loser.

Look, you're being really harsh. I'm not trying to say I've had it worse than anybody else. I haven't. But pain isn't a competition, is it? I mean, if I have a headache but somebody else has a brain tumour, my pain doesn't just disappear, does it? It's not like I've got some weird sort of symbiotic connection to the poor sod with the tumour, and my pain lessens the worse theirs gets.

You're talking nonsense again. This is what you do. You bamboozle people with this waffle and throw in a big word or two and people think you're astute, or clever, and you're not, you've just learned how to fool people. Take your mask off and let people see what's really under there. Different story, isn't it?

That's what I'm saying, though. I'm willing to take the mask off. I don't mind people seeing what's going on inside my skull. You're the one who said nobody would be interested.

What are you listening to me for? I'm a voice a couple of inches inside your left ear. I don't even know what I'm going to say until it's left my mouth. Not that I have a mouth, of course. That's why I use yours sometimes.

We're getting sidetracked. All I'm saying is that I've suffered with mental health issues all my life. Depression. Mania. Addiction. Obsessive Compulsive Disorder. Suicidal ideation. I see stuff that isn't there. I've been on medication since I was 17. I make a living from my imagination, but my imagination is the thing that's almost driven me over the edge more times than I can count.

You're whining again. Nobody likes a whiner. Have a drink. You deserve a drink.

It's not whining, is it? I'm being honest. People are supposed to do that. We're in the age of being kind to yourself. We're meant to let people work through their pain and make allowances for their past traumas and make sure we don't trigger bad memories or shatter their self-esteem, or ...

That's working, is it? People are being understanding of one another's mental health problems, are they?

Well, there are some great quotes on social media ...

Nobody gives a shit, David. Not really. Not about you, anyway. You keep making the same mistakes — believing people when they tell you that sensitivity is sexy and that you're in a safe place to cry. You've tried to open up and those closest to you have weaponized your sensitivity and stabbed it right through your fucking heart.

That's not true. When I fell off the wagon there were loads of people reaching out, saying they were here if I needed them. They really cared.

Bollocks. You said the same when that bloke said he was going through a hard time. You said you were there for him if he needed it. If he'd called you'd have let it go to Voicemail.

No, that's not true. I do care about people. I want people to feel better.

No, you want to have helped people get better. That's the difference. It has to be about you and how great you are.

I'm not great! I have chronic self-loathing.

While also thinking you're amazing, under-appreciated and have been generally short-changed by life.

Not true. I'm happy.

Bollocks.

I am. I'm satisfied, at least. I have a partner I love, and children I adore, and I've achieved what I set out to achieve as a novelist.

Have you? Ticked all the boxes, have you? Might as well save yourself time, then. Might as well jump off something before you fuck it all up. Only way is down.

You are so bleak.

I'm a realist. You used to be as well. You saw through it all — all that saccharine, touchy-feely, namy-pamby, treacly bullshit...

That's very hateful language.

It's not even a whisper of what I feel. You remember it, David. The rage. The absolute and overwhelming hate.

I remember the sadness. The misery. I remember feeling as though I were wrapped in black plastic and sinking into a lake of oil and sulphur.

Yeah, very pretty. Lovely imagery. But it's all made up. You know that. Your brain only works when you're painting pretty pictures. You make depression sound romantic. Cinematic. You're going to make people worse.

Please...

Please. Christ you're pathetic. You should have a drink. Or go find Nicola. When she doesn't respond to you in exactly the right way, you can turn it into a braided rope to whip yourself with. If you're lucky, she'll be in a foul mood and will jerk away when you try to kiss her neck. You can smash that one into your cheekbone for days, you ugly fuck.

Don't. I don't do that.

You're feeling sick now? Oh Christ, you baby! Go on, throw it up before you embarrass yourself. Go hurl now before anybody sees. Empty yourself. A proper purging. Make your eyes pop and get the capillaries in your cheeks to burst like ripe fruit.

It's just a way to control things. I'd rather be sick on my own terms.

Or how about you're not sick at all, like everybody else – like all the people who go through life without messing things up time and again. Proper grown-ups. People who've got their shit together.

How can I get my shit together? I'm mentally ill.

Oh, that's rich. Convenient too. And this from the man who hates excuses?

It's not an excuse. It's a diagnosis. I'm bi-polar, at least.

So that absolves you of all the other stuff, does it? You're four months behind on the rent! You've been bankrupt twice. Your children have opened the door to bailiffs and coppers. You can't afford to put fuel in the car and even if you could, you've lost your licence for failing to have insurance. Why was that again? Yeah – you couldn't afford the insurance.

I live a different way. I do my best. I take care of the people who matter to me …

Do you? You walked out on your wife and daughter. You spent 14 years drunk out of your skull…

No, that's not right. I was a good Dad. I am a good Dad.

But you were drinking a bottle of whisky a day …

Not that you would notice. I became an internationally best-selling novelist while living that way …

And a thief and a cheat and a liar. You lost it all. Spent it on holidays and wine and picking up everybody else's bill so you could feel like a big-shot. And what toll did it take on your daughter, eh?

She's brilliant.

Wrong.

Sorry, they are brilliant. I can't get my pronouns in order. But they are brilliant.

You're an embarrassment. A loser. You're clever enough to think your way around the bits that don't fit your narrative, but deep down, you know you're the fucking devil. You're the worst person in the world. You're acid. You're bile. You're a fucking tumour …

Stop it. I'm trying. I never stop trying.

Save them all the bother. Just stop. You believe in God. He'll understand. You might get a special type of afterlife where everybody tells you you're brilliant every day and you're taller than 5ft 8.

No. People need me.

Ha! Who?

Nicola. The kids …

Yeah, you're irreplaceable? You. A fat little loser with glasses and a bad chest. You, who has to borrow money from the kids' birthday cards to be able to get stuff for packed lunches …

It will come together. It will. Something will turn up. It has before …

Loser…

No, I swear, I'm worth trusting in.

Loser…

I'm a good writer. I try. I don't quit.

Loser …

I'm what I set out to be.

Go on. A bottle of whisky, all the ibuprofen you can get your hands on. Lay back against the tree and let go. There might be a plaque there one day. The funeral will be beautiful. Think of all those people in tears, telling stories about what an amazing guy you were. It would be a right kick in the dick for those who doubted you, too.

I'm not like that any more.

So you're not mentally ill any more? Better get a job then. A proper job, with regular hours and a wage and some kind of tax contribution…

I'm a writer. I teach people how to write. I give talks. I'm doing okay.

Bankruptcy would suggest not. Sales figures aren't exactly cheerful reading …

That's why I'm trying this! All this pain. All this real-life experience oif listening to you. All the voices and the visions and the impulses and the mistake after mistake after mistake …

You cynical fucker, David. You really are trying to make money out of misery, aren't you?

It's my misery, I can do what I want with it.

You're worse than I am. You're going to Hell.

I know. But I know that you're not really there. And I am. And I'm getting better.

7.

Forever In Blue Genes

I'm seven or eight or nine or ten, and Dad is getting sad. He stares into space a lot and doesn't always respond when I say his name. He glowers at stuff, just gazing into something or nothing as if he's reading some invisible script. I'm worried, inasmuch as I worry about anything that isn't school or football or telly. He's a grown-up, so it's probably normal, though it's not, is it? Not really. There's this cloud around him, like the haze you get above a candle. I imagine him sitting so still that he ends up covered in lichen and cobwebs and turns into a graveyard statue. When he notices me watching he just says something silly, like 'hishnabilba', which is a word he's made up, and which used to make us laugh when he used it on Mam.

Dad getting sad isn't something we talk about very much. He works hard, does Dad. Trying to make something of himself. He's gone from a manual job to an office role and seems to be doing well. He's always had a good brain, according to Nana, my mam's mum. She knew as soon as she met him that he had a good head on his shoulders. It's hardly surprising that it's tiring him out and he's not really in the mood to run about in the back garden or sit and watch me play with my toys. He needs five minutes' peace.

I first hear the word 'Depression' in a conversation I'm not supposed to be listening to. It's said like 'Flu' or 'Mumps', with a proper capital letter and appropriate levels of whispered solemnity. We're at Uncle P 's house and they've all forgotten I'm here. I can sit very quietly if there's a chance of gossip. Mam's telling my auntie all about Dad's sadness. She wants him to see somebody. He's 'very, very low'. She can't seem to cheer him up. He sits with his headphones on listening to music and it's like he's somewhere a thousand miles away in his head. Or he loses his temper over nothing. She's trying to think of things they can look forward to, but she's got two boys to bring up and a house to worry about and who has the money to plan big fancy stuff when there's barely enough money to last the month or pay for football boots? He gets giddy too, she says. Just behaves like he's not right in the head. He says stupid things and embarrasses her and is properly awkward in company. We're going on holiday with Nana and Grandad soon and she doesn't think he's going to come. He doesn't want to bring everybody down.

Uncle P translates, later. Depression is 'extreme sadness'. It's like being in the worst mood ever, times by a thousand. It's like everybody you've ever loved has died, and it's your fault. It's an illness. It's like feeling totally miserable and numb all at once. Some people, he confides, get so miserable that they even want to die. Nobody knows where it comes from, but P knows he'll get through it. After all, he's got his boys to pull him through.

I'm nine or ten when Dad takes the overdose. Turns out he's had himself a bit on the side for the past few months. I know what a bit on the side is, as it's what Dirty Den has in EastEnders. Dirty Den is cool, though. And Dad's Dad.

I find out later that it all started out innocently enough. Her bloke died unexpectedly, dropping dead right in front of her. She works for Dad, and she doesn't have anybody to help her through the grief. Dad, all heart, goes to help her out, doing some jobs around the house and generally being a decent chap. He mows the lawn. Puts up a shelf or two. I don't know when it becomes something more but I do know that he's staying out late and not coming out with us at the weekends like he did before. He's at work a lot. He's telling Mam that she's neurotic a lot more than he used to. His accent's weird. He isn't talking like himself.

One day he asks his mam and dad to drop him off at the far side of the city, near enough to where his colleague lives. They don't know who he's talking about or where he's going, so Mam just comes out with it and tells them he's going to see his girlfriend. It all gets a bit unpleasant, but I don't see it, as I'm upstairs with my brother playing computer games or reading Enid Blyton, and real life seems far too real to engage with.

And one morning I'm in the living room, cross-legged on the floor, watching something I've seen a million times before. I'm driving a toy car along the pattern in the rug. Things are normal for the last time.

Mam comes in with her serious face on. Her eyes are wide but the pupils are tiny. Her lips are grey.

"You need to go up to Nana's. Your dad's taken an overdose. I'm ringing the ambulance now."

It's all a blur, for a bit. I cycle up to Nana's. There's no real drama in my head, I'm just a bit bamboozled by it all. I know overdoses are something that people take when they want to kill themselves and I know that depressives sometimes get so unhappy that they would rather be dead than alive. But that doesn't seem like Dad. He's been better. He's been weird, but not as gloomy. I've heard people call it 'the coward's way out' though I don't know if I agree with that. It seems quite a scary thing to do.

I've become a bit of an expert on suicide, as it goes. There were leaflets at the doctors and I read them folded inside my comics, filling my head with images of swinging corpses and open pill bottles, open veins and bodies pancaked on the pavement. I find it fascinating. Ten-year-olds love death, don't they? Gory stuff. Even the word 'splatter' is fun to say. And there's something weirdly intoxicating about knowing something that belongs so firmly in the adult world. I feel like I did when Stephen Cullen first told me the real word for fanny. Suicide's like that – something forbidden, but deliciously 'wow'. It sounds awful but I can see the logic. When you're so unhappy that you can't stand to take another breath, it makes sense to put an end to it all. If you're hungry, you eat. If you're bursting for the toilet you relieve yourself where you can. If you hate life, death is just next door. Whatever comes next, even if it's nothing, must eventually seem like an infinitely better bet. It makes me sad to imagine him feeling like that. It makes me sad to think how bad he'll feel when he wakes up and realises he's still alive. But I'm oddly thrilled to learn that if it does all get too much, you don't actually have to go on with it. It's like reading Lord of the Rings, in a way. You can just call it a day if you can't face another page.

Nana's on the phone a lot during the hours that follow. I watch telly and talk to grandad and lose myself in the sawdust and poster-paint of the workshop, helping as he makes a bird table or a Roman centurion shield or a miniature violin or one of the mad projects that he's usually got on the go. He's semi-retired, is Grandad, and keeps himself busy. Plays saxophone and clarinet in jazz bands. Draws.

Makes up silly poems. We don't talk about Dad all day and by tea-time I've actually forgotten what's happened. I feel a bit of a fraud when Auntie Sue turns up with my brother and everybody tells me, in breathless tones, that Dad's okay, he's going to be fine; he's tired and a bit out of it but there shouldn't be any long term damage. He should be home in a couple of days, or maybe he'll go to stay with his Mam and Dad for a bit, we're not sure, we'll just play it by ear, but you need to keep everybody's spirits up and be strong, yeah …

Mam and me have the briefest of chats. She needs me to be the best big brother I can be. He, too, needs to be a big brave lad while everybody decides what to do next. And me? I'm going to have to be the man of the house. Be strong. Take on some of the responsibility. Don't go making things worse with any of my silliness. Keep everybody as cheerful as I can. Make them laugh, no matter what. Don't, just don't, make it any worse.

I find out somewhere down the line that the catalyst for his grand exit was the fact that his fancy piece had got cold feet. He was willing to commit to a new life with her and she wasn't sure it was what she wanted. It pushed him over the edge. He came home, took umpteen painkillers, then went to bed. He told Mam what he'd done the next morning. Then, and now, I find myself wonder-ing whether she felt tempted to just close the door on him and let him have what he wanted. It speaks well of her that she called 999.

Ten-year-old me doesn't know what to make of any of it. It's exciting, certainly. My mate up the road knows more about it all than I do. He can't believe my Mam hasn't been round to see the fancy piece and kicked the shit out of her. We're not like that, I explain. And Mam's the size of a sparrow, like me. David rarely gets to beat Goliath, even if he has righteousness upon his side. He asks how I feel about Dad. I answer as well as I can. I'm not cross at him. I'm bamboozled, really. It's all very confusing. I get in trouble for telling the neighbor the truth about why there had been an ambulance at the house. 'Dad tried to kill himself. He'd been seeing this woman and she ended it so he tried to kill himself. But he's on the mend'. He doesn't quite know where to look. Seems shocked, which suggests that we're not that kind of family.

He's in bed for a while. I pop upstairs to see him now and again but we don't talk about what happened. We never talk about what happened. He gets into therapy and gets on the right medication and goes back to being glib and silly. He gets promotions at work and starts a Master's degree. He keeps himself busy and never actually moves out.

And then I'm 13 and I'm seeing things and hearing things. I'm so un-happy I can barely catch my breath. I'm having panic attacks when I leave the house. I feel sick all the time – throwing up at the slightest variation from my routine; angry and hateful and desperate to be somebody else. Dad and me don't talk about his own experiences. Ever. I hear him telling Mam that this is all because of him; that he's defective, that he's done this.

Years later, when he leaves Mam for the same fancy piece, I've just left my own wife and our six-month-old child. For a while, we talk like two men. He doesn't know what it's all about either. Doesn't know what women want. Doesn't expect anybody to un-derstand him. If he fell in a barrel of tits he'd come out sucking his thumb. He tells me that he knows I understand because I've been through it. It's better than the last time he came down, when I was still throwing up every five minutes and unable to eat because my throat was so swollen from holding back tears and refusing to cry. I don't know if he's ever seen me cry. I know I've never seen him.

It's not a sore that festers. Or maybe it is. I have a hard time working out what are thoughts and what are feelings. I hope I don't trace my every problem back to that brief run-in with pills and blue lights and death. I know he was going through hell. I just wish he'd tried it because of the depression and not because his fancy piece had turned him down. If he was going to leave me and Mam and my little brother, I'd have liked it to be for a more noble reason than a broken heart. As an adult, I see things differently. But not much.

He and the fancy piece are still together. Very much in love, or so it seems. I don't see much of him, though I'd like to. I'd like to ask him a lot of questions. He probably knows that, which is why he's so rarely here. He was who I reached out to the last time my brain twisted itself up in knots. He didn't really know what to say. He wants an easy life,

I think, and he can't relax around me and the fancy piece at the same time in case one version of events be undermined in front of the other.

Mam's easier to talk to. She's always clear that he was a really good Father who loved me and my brother very much. I remind him of himself, apparently. And he's very proud of me.

I sent him a text message yesterday, asking if he was home so me and the littlest could go see him for a catch-up. He's in Wales, apparently. Must be nice.

8

Aren't You Better Yet?

Because I'm honest about my loose wiring and my bouts of absolute bona fide gosh-he's-off-his-head madness, people ask me questions about mental health, mental ill-health, and what the bloody hell they should say to somebody who's so mired in depression that they haven't got the strength to pull their hand free from a tube of Pringle's.

This is a tricky one for me. I'm a great believer in free speech. I'm also a knobhead who thinks everybody should be able to take a joke and who uses humour as a release valve for tension and unpleasantness.

So …

Maybe you should say what you like. Maybe your friend needs to hear some unvarnished truth. Tell them they don't look depressed. Tell them everybody gets down sometimes. Tell them that it's time to pull their socks up and put on their big-boy/big-girl pants and damn well show the world who's boss. You've got the right to express your feelings and I've got the right to think you're an arsehole as a consequence.

I can't help thinking that If you're going to soften yourself for anybody, you should do it for the people you purport to love, and who are really, really doing their damnedest to drag themselves out of an abyss of pain and suffering that you cannot even begin to comprehend. If you're going to concern yourself with 'the right thing', do it in honour of those you care about, if and when they are suddenly struck insensible by the great lump-hammer of unbearable sadness. While we're at it, don't punch people made of glass, or ask people made of sugar if they fancy a walk in the rain.

This shouldn't come as much of a revelation, but it pays to watch your words with depressed people. Bite your tongue if you feel the impulse to dispense some down-to-earth, speak-as-I-find, matter-of-fact piece of tough love. Please. We're sensitive, you see. That's why we're so endlessly fascinating and utterly unbearable. But in the bad times, the least little thing really could prove too much. We tend to obsess about things said and unsaid. We can create whole movies of sub-text and transcribe reams of somebody else's internal monologue based on an eye-roll or an over-long sigh. We hate ourselves, you see. And we know we're an unimaginable burden. For all that social media is slick with greasy platitudes preaching about the importance of patience, compassion and understanding regarding mental health disorders, in reality most people get bored pretty quickly once you actually start to exhibit the signs of one. It's hardly surprising. Is there anything more frustrating than somebody else's abject despair? Christ, who wants to be around that? Who wants to spend time with somebody who looks like they're on the brink of tears all the time? Life's precious and short and popping to see that gloomy sod with the deathwish is hardly a recipe for a good time. Truly, I do understand. But do be careful about making things, y'know …worse. You may be saying the things that were said to you, but there's a good chance that the things that were said to you were the ramblings of an insensitive twat. You have not thought about your loved one's problems' more than they have. They're not in the market for advice. They're in an abyss of absolute wretchedness and you telling them to 'think about the kids' is akin to asking your quadruple-amputee neighbor whether they fancy a wrestle. As far as I'm concerned, using the phrase 'man up' should be listed as a hate crime.

So, suggestions? Well, the best thing you can do is imagine yourself consumed by a misery from which there seems no escape, and then think about the things you might like to hear if you were in that situation. That's called 'empathy'. It's gone out of fashion but it used to be quite popular.

Anyway, never doubt that the scorn, loathing and disgust I pour upon myself in my dark times is vastly in excess of any that could be thrown my way by somebody else. But that being said, I'm still capable of losing hours of my life to ruminating on some well-intentioned banality.

So, probably best not say:

"We all get down sometimes."

"You can't carry on like this."

"This is getting a bit much."

"You really need to take a good look at yourself."

"You're just like everybody else."

"Look what this is doing to the people who love you."

That last one is the worst. In the wrong head, it's permission, nay a positive instruction, to remove yourself from the lives of your loved ones by jumping off something high and slitting a vein before hitting the ground.

The other banalities probably come from a good place. I've doubtless said them myself from time to time. Other people's wretchedness can, of course, be deeply infuriating. You'd need to be the Dalai Lama to sustain your patience and consideration for every single moment of somebody else's depression. But do your best. On some level, it's appreciated.

And if you can't think of anything to say, try some of the things that nobody's ever said to me, but I'd love to be told more often.

"I'm not going to lose my faith in you."

"I'm so proud of the steps you're taking."

"Whatever happens, I'll always be here."

"Take all the time that you need".

"This isn't your fault."

"The world would be so much poorer without you."

People have said endlessly supportive, flattering and downright desperate things to me during my darkest times. I'll always be appreciative of the place from which these good intentions flow. But most of the time they amount to telling a fallen pensioner to overcome their broken legs and dislocated hips by getting up and having a bash with a hula hoop. For me, "You need to get over this" is up there with telling a blind person that it's you or the dog. Patience, tenderness and hope are your best friends. Sorry if they don't come naturally. But if you love somebody enough to want them to get well, you can find that reservoir of forbearance inside you, I promise.

If bouts of sincerity make you feel icky (and that might be something for you to talk about in therapy), you may feel the urge to crack a joke in order to lift the general mood of perennial gloom. I'll let you judge that for yourself based on the person in question but I've certainly found that humour can still be appreciated by even the most unhappy of people. Depression is, after all, quite ridiculous. Surreal, even. Your brain turns against you, your soul turns to wet dust and suddenly you're drowning in a great barrel full of eels and shit and toxic bile and you can't conceive of ever having laughed before or knowing happiness ever again and all you want to do is not exist, or never have existed, and you can't breathe through the sheer cloying despair. In such moments, who doesn't love a one-liner?

But, that being said, I've talked a few potential suicides back from the figurative brink and I will admit to occasionally trying to get through the wall of sadness with the chisel of silliness. I did once use the following, to my continued delight:

"Fine, you want to die. But that's such a waste. Can't we register you as a lethal weapon and send you into dangerous situations?"

That worked, actually. So far.

But listening is more important than talking. Don't try and be a therapist. Don't counsel. Just listen when they want to talk. Little steps are all you can ask for. But given time, they can take you quite a way from danger.

Jesus, that sounded so saccharine it turned my stomach.

9

Could You Call Us Back If You Really Do Kill Yourself?

It's 2014, or thereabouts.

I'm going insane again.

This is how it feels.

I am a toothache. That's probably the best way I can describe it, and if it doesn't quite fit, I promise that I'll be up until 3am, chewing my tongue to paste and loathing my damnable self for not being better at comparisons.

Over the years I have come up with a lot of lyrical ways to describe living with chronic depression and they all say pretty much the same thing. It's like wearing damp clothes. It's that feeling when you've just got out the shower and started sweating again and don't know whether you are smearing water or perspiration around on your skin with the scratchy bath towel. It's like being trapped forever in the moment between breaking your toes and the pain reaching your brain. But most of all, it's a fucking toothache; a cold, penetrating hollow kind of throb that blunts every other sense and seems to emit a high, keening whine just outside the range of human hearing.

Still with me? No. Fair enough. Not many people are still on board at this point. More fool them for asking 'so, how are you?' They tend to move away, or pull a face that suggests they were only asking out of politeness. Those who do make an effort to understand have little to offer in the way of help. They offer comfort in platitudes about how we all have our low moments and the darkest hour comes just before the dawn. Or they tell me about an aunt or uncle who suffered depression all their life and eventually stuck their head in the deep fat fryer. Better yet, I am offered the strangest of compliments. I suffer with mental illness because it is the flip side of my creativity. My misery is my penance for my gifts. Sure, Van Gogh hacked off his ear but boy, he was a whiz with the colour yellow...

Why am I telling you this? Well, I have nobody else to tell. Not a professional, anyways. It's been almost a year since I was assessed by an NHS psychiatrist who declared that cognitive behavioural therapy was urgently required and that I was in the grip of a mental episode characterised by chronic depression, hallucinations (both auditory and visual) and was exhibiting symptoms of borderline personality disorder. None of that sounds particularly positive. I'd go as far as to say that, on paper, I sound as if I shouldn't be allowed access to anything sharper than a bar of soap.

I've been waiting for an appointment ever since. Apparently, the waiting is simply to be endured. They're very busy, which is hardly surprising, considering one in four people suffers with a mental health problem of one degree or another. I can pay to see a private shrink, which I have done in the past. But at an average of 50 quid an hour, it's a luxury that I can't really afford.

In the meantime, I've got worse. Three months ago, drunk out of my mind and screaming with absolute despair, I came as close as I ever have to simply stopping. To switching myself off. To becoming nothing. Only the love of my children and the fact that I was only halfway through the new series of Game of Thrones, persuaded me not to do it. Instead, I chose to ask for help. To puddle at the feet of my loved ones and say 'I can't do this any more'. Support was forthcoming. Even in the face of their own sadness at seeing me in such a state, they offered me whatever I may need to get well.

My partner sat cursing at the computer for hours, trying to find out what to do when a loved one suffers a chronic mental collapse. The advice was interesting. It seems that what you are supposed to do is go and see your doctor. They will refer you to mental health services who will assess you and put you on a waiting list.

We knew this already. We'd done this already. Months ago. I had to speak to a chirpy girl called Candy on the telephone and grade my self-loathing out of ten. She came out with the memorable line that I sounded like my life was pretty good and wished she could be in my shoes ...

Surely there was some other provision - some emergency care. My partner phoned one of the mental health charities and managed to speak to a human being. I was already on the waiting list, explained my partner. "He's been waiting months," she said, and I heard the helplessness in her voice. "He's getting worse. I'm genuinely scared for him…"

The advice, when we found it, had clearly been written by Joseph Heller and George Orwell - a Catch 22 circa 1984. If I was already in the system, I would have a phone number for the community psychiatric team, but given that I wasn't a patient yet, that wouldn't apply. I could go to Casualty, they suggested, but there would be the risk of me being sectioned under the Mental Health Act. The only other suggestion, related time and again on online message forums that dripped with frustration, was that I get myself arrested so the police or magistrate could fast-track me into the system.

As it is, I have gone for the option that this Government seems keen on instituting as policy. I am suffering, and keeping going. I am falling deeper and deeper inside myself. I am living in a toothache. I am waiting for my appointment with a counsellor and trying not to lose sight of myself along the way.

I'm not the sort of chap who asks for help. Few men are very good at admitting they can't cope. But I'm admitting it. I can't get myself better on my own. I love the idea of a positive mental attitude chasing the blues away but you wouldn't expect a cancer sufferer to think themselves well. I have a chemical imbalance in my brain and an artistic soul that looks, in the eye of my imagination, like a pit of tar and eels. I'm 5ft 8" of despair. 15st of self-loathing. And it seems I've just got to put up with it.

I find myself wishing there were still asylums. I'd take cold baths, restraints and electric shock treatment in a heartbeat. It has to be better than nothing at all.

10

Just a Teenage Dirtbag

'95, I think. Britpop and Tarantino and which-Spice-Girl-do-you-fancy-the-most. Purple hair and a celtic cross; an earring and Adidas Gazelles. I've got a girlfriend from the other side of the city and every-body reckons we're perfect for each other. She's artistic. Passionate. Broodingly enigmatic. Her dad died when she was younger so she's fabulously messed up. She cuts herself unless she remembers not to. I'm infatuated, of course. She's the most interesting person I've ever met. She's so unbelievably talented. She could go far and I think I might die if she doesn't promise to take me with her. She's in love with me and says it a lot. She seems to think I could be somebody special, given half a chance. She sees the sadness in me and thinks I should use it as fuel. Thinks the letters I write her are beautiful. We had our first kiss moment after she saw me trying not to cry. There's something significant in that but I don't yet know what it is.

She knows that I get sad. I see things. I write poems and songs and would like to be an author or a rock star or something in-between. She knows I have a temper but hate confrontation. She's more worldly-wise than me, or at least, there's a sophisti-cation to her thinking that I'm not familiar with. She's heard of people I haven't. She mentions feminist poets and iconic artists the way my usual crowd mention guitar players and footballers.

She's seen me upset. She's seen how hard I try not to come apart. She's of the opinion that some professional help might be a good idea, before I start making self-destructive decisions or letting my moments of hyper-manic ebullience persuade me to test my strength against a moving vehicle. She's witnessed my little rituals; my obsessive need to touch every side of the picture frames in my bedroom,; to lock and unlock the front door; to turn right then left; to use my fingertip as a pencil and write absurd scribblings on my jeans as I walk along. I make room in my life for these little gestures. To not perform them is to invite ruin. To forget to dismount from a flight of steps with my left foot first, is to court annihilation. I don't throw anything away any more. Every scrap of fluff and strip of paper needs to be carefully collected and curated. If I catch sight of an odd number, somebody I love is going to die. If I take my socks off out of order then I'm never going to make a success of myself. When she asks me about it, I try and make light. But she knows about sadness and ways to cope with it and she knows I've got a problem. The doctor does too, now. She's a nice GP. Big and floral and motherly. 17's a tough age, she says. Hormones, the jump to adulthood; the fear of what comes next – it's enough to make anybody question their sanity. But I'm doing well, aren't I? A trainee journalist on the local newspaper at just 17 years-of-age. I must have some serious gumption about me to have even applied. She's right, I suppose. Though I only really applied because Mam wouldn't stop going on about it and because the thought of staying at school then heading off to university filled me with absolute dread. Me? At university? Among people who really understand the things I pretend to? Fuck that.

I seem to be getting the hang of the job and haven't been unmasked as a fraud just yet, but life has taken a weird turn. I'm spending my days surrounded by proper grown-ups; adults who don't have to pretend they're something other than they are. It's full of people who are clever and naughty at once. I feel at home, and also horribly out of my depth. I'm in a band, too. We're doing well. I play saxophone and nobody has realized that I'm shit, or that every member of my family has more musical ability in a single toe than I do in my whole, achingly desperate body. I enjoy the practices though, and my bandmates are all artistic and bohemian and mentally skewed. Mam hints that I'm only struggling with my mental health because I've seen how much attention that our guitarist and drummer got when they sprained their brains and ended up having brief sojourns at the mental hospital. I'm just trying to be trendy.

But here I am. 17 and bleak as Hell and waiting to see my psychologist. The session takes place at the Family Planning Clinic, which is odd, because I was here a few weeks back having heard that this is the place to come for free condoms. It's also the sexual health clinic, where my mate endured an invasive procedure involving the shaft of his penis and something not unlike a cocktail umbrella. So in my mind it's very much a one-stop shop for the scraping out of all unwanted and decidedly putrid matter.

I'm nervous, of course. The voices in my head are having a blast. It's all very Jim Henson inside my mind: Muppets and Fraggles and those grotesque furry puppets from Labyrinth and Dark Crystal. They terrify me, and they live inside my skull. They laugh a lot: high and manic. They dine upon one another and treat me to the sound of tooth breaking bone and bone breaking tooth. It never stops. Never. Not ever. If you need to understand it, think of the times you've seen a picture in the clouds or a stain or the flickering of the fire – the way one thing suddenly becomes something else. That's constant for me. Every single thing is also something repulsive and animated and performing just for me. You tell me they're not real and I believe you. But they heard you too and they think you're a dickhead.

His name's Todd, apparently. Sensibly dressed, apart from the unnecessarily zany socks. Youngish, for somebody so eminently qualified to poke around inside my head. Slightly plump, in that glossy, oil-painted cherub kind of way. He's friendly and a wee bit too jovial in his manner, though that's probably my fault. I can't help but give glib answers to earnest questions and he's just following my lead. And how else to perform? How else to be but this version of myself. I've got character, you see. I'm memorable. I've got the gift of the gab. I'm funny and clever and I damn well need to show that off, which is why I don't really draw breath between sentences and have got a repertoire of killer lines and pithy, off-the-cuff comebacks.

I don't take much unpicking. I'm very, very sad. I have no energy. I have to will myself to attempt even the most simple of tasks. I'm filled with fear and hate. I don't recognize myself any more. Nothing makes me feel better. Food tastes of nothingness and I can't stop throwing up. And yes, there's some family history with considering. My parents had me very young, you see. And they do their best. I'm not blaming anybody, but it's so fucking unfair, isn't it? To put me in the middle of this family that was totally unsuited to the job of raising somebody without a single redeeming quality. They try their best, they really do, but how can anybody be expected to love this, to be proud of this, to believe that this monstrous specimen will ever become something other than the vile, undeserving, prick who oozes and slithers through their lives and sucks up their love and patience like a full sponge.

He's rather unmoved by it all. He's heard better and worse. He wants to talk to me about both sides of my family. I make a comment about Mam's side being in full colour and Dad's being black and white. Mam's side talk to each other and share their feelings, up to a point. Dad's don't. It's hard, I concur. Hard to reconcile the two sides of my nature. Not for me, of course – I know I'm all Dad. But my brother, he's a bit of both and it messes with him…

An hour goes by pretty quickly. I waste too much of it on chit-chat about the band. He betrays a wisp of a stutter at one point. He asks me about my diet and whether I'm eating enough and I answer that yes, I am. I don't tell him that I vomit after every meal, just to be sure that I won't be sick in front of anybody later in the day. He asks about my sex life and I tell him that I have one, and that I've been sexually active since I was uncommonly young, and that it's more important to me to be thought as as an exceptional lover than to reach any kind of satisfaction of my own. We're just getting on to ambition when he says we're done for the week. He has no doubt I'm suffering from Depression and he can prescribe something if I feel I need it. He doesn't think I'm a danger to myself or to others. He wants me to go back to the doctor if I feel no real improvement in mood within a month.

The voice won't let me leave. It wants me to ask the question that has been drilling into the fleshy matter of my brain. I keep getting hot ears, you see. One or both of my ears keep turning crimson and I know, deep down, that it's because my girlfriend is telling her friends and family my deepest secrets, and laughing at me, and trying to work out how to tell me that I'm a worthless little loser who needs to be wrapped in a sack and thrown in a pond like the pitiful runt that I am.

What does it mean if your ears keep burning, I ask, trying to keep it light while simultaneously pleading with this mental health professional to give me something to soothe myself with.

He's all smiles as he tells me that it just means somebody's talking about me. Left for Love, Right for Spite.

I smile my thanks as I leave, feeling the flimsy scaffolds within me begin to topple and fall in upon themselves. He knows nothing. Doesn't understand. Didn't even see me glancing up and down, left and right, watching as the blood-red goblins wrestled and fought and fucked between his shoes.

It's another few months before my brain pops. The band members move into a house together and I let myself in one blustery weekday afternoon, sauntering in the back door as I always do when they're with me and we're all carrying our instruments and six-packs and chatting about our perfect tour-bus. They're not home. Their housemate is. Half-dressed and disheveled in the kitchen, thinking he has the place to himself. He housemate isn't as Bohemian as they are. He hates the fact his spare room is now a hang-out for half a dozen long-haired losers. He reacts poorly to his unexpected visitor. He's sick of it. He thinks I'm mouthy. Too big for my boots. No fucking manners. I've just walked in through his back door without the courtesy of a knock and now I'm telling him to chill, not to get so wound up, not to push my buttons ...

He's a big lad. Older than me. Doesn't appreciate the lip, or the stupid smirk I'm giving him. I'm scared, so I smirk more. I feel like a prat so I say more witty, cutting things to compensate.

He gets in my face.

He calls me a 'little shit'.

He tries to throw me out.

And everything goes a funny colour and the world turns red and black.

Later, back at home, the voices in my head are absolutely stone-cold quiet. I feel elated. Now would be a perfect time to die.

Later, I get a call from the drummer in the band. to say not to worry, he's going to be okay, and he's heard from the guitarist that I've trashed my room, and they're worrying about me. They'll come over, if they can get a car, but they've got loads of other shit going on. Their housemate wants them all to leave and they've got nowhere else to go. He's an arsehole, deserve what he got, whatever that was, and they've told him I'm off my fucking head and that I he doesn't need the world of trouble I'll bring down on him if he makes a meal of it.

I still don't know what I did.

The bass player ends up camping with his girlfriend in a field near my house. They're woken by a herd of cows and think they make have done something to their brains by pitching directly beneath power lines. It'll be fine, they reckon. Glastonbury soon. Something will turn up, it usually does. Mam gives them breakfast when I tell them they're nearby: hunkered down inside an orange tent on the edge of the suburban housing estate; two hippies and their worldly goods, playing the bongos and welcoming the sun. She likes them. Lets them shower. They're good for me, even if they're not her cup of tea. Dad makes them laugh. My little brother, 13 now, looks at these intruders in our house as if they're visitors from space. He likes them too. Rebellious and naughty and charming and talented and all the selfsame things that I am and which make me so damn objectionable to the people I love.

When I see the next psychologist, the word 'depression' is written on the top of the report she's holding. I can read it upside down. So can the monsters, as they hang by their toes and pull goblin faces and tell me that she's trying to trick me; that she can't be trusted; that I don't need anybody – I have them.

When my girlfriend leaves me, it's for somebody with less emotional baggage.

12.

The Dying of The Light

Now.

I wake her up some time around 10.30am. She asked for an hour but I always give her a little bit more. I hold her mug of tea as if it were flowers.

She's asleep on her side, facing away, hands clasped softly together on the pillow as if she's praying. Her legs are curled up under her. The bedroom curtains are open, the sash window all the way down. Ground floor, slap-bang on a busy hiking path and neither of us give a damn about people peeping in.

I stand for a few moments and drink her in: My Nicola the way I'm Her David: bed-headed and lovely in a room that echoes with birdsong, and which smells of us.

It will drain me, this gladness. These little bursts of golden delight have an uncanny ability to bring me down. When good times come, so too the sense of unworthiness. For there is surely a price to be paid for these fleeting blessings. To suffer is to store up credit, I tell myself, when I'm being unkind. To endure is to prove oneself noteworthy; resilient, commendable. To suffer cruelties and vicissitudes is to guarantee a place in some distant Paradise.

I know these thoughts to be wrong and cruel and symptoms of my illness.

But I think them nonetheless.

And so we talk for a while. Cuddle. I breathe her in, my nose seeking that place behind her ear where her scent seems to live. I make her laugh. We share her tea. She looks like Boudicca with her bright red tresses, though she's got that 'escaped mental patient' vibe going on thanks to the plain white T-shirt and stripy pyjama trousers. She went out in the field like looking this last night: trying to recover the bloody dog. The middle child was out too: hopeless in her pyjamas and borrowed hiking boots, watching as Bailey - her one responsibility - disappeared into the next field and proceeded to anoint herself with dead rabbit and sheep shit. The littlest came out to help before it was all over and done with. Welly boots and a red fur coat: bare-arsed and giggling as she chased the labradoodle through the long grass and told her sister she was a doofus for letting her off the lead. There were more laughs than the situation called for, and it was me who lost my temper. I'd asked for help, you see. Let somebody else do it. Own silly fault.

She's doing well, is Nicola. The new therapist seems to have the measure of her. She won't let her keep falling into the same traps she's fallen into before. Won't let her get away with being horrid to herself. She's insisting she examine all of her impulses and suspicions and throw away the ones that are either a load of bollocks or singularly unhelpful. There's four decades of self-loathing to chisel through so it won't happen overnight but for now, we're certainly making more good memories than bad. Strawberry picking, yesterday. A couple of tantrums but nothing that would suggest either of us is a danger to ourselves. Irritation never became fury. Disappointment stopped short of absolute despair.

It could all change at a moment's notice, but that's the risk we all take, isn't it? And she's worth it. Worth all of it. I knew she had issues when we got together. There were more red flags than at a Wales match. Same with me, I guess. She knew I saw things and heard things and got very, very sad. She's tried to off herself. I'd always wanted to. I'd betrayed people. Done my fair share of bad things. She, too, unrolled a scroll of her perceived misdeeds, sins and indiscretions. Here, we told one another. Look at my entirety. See all that I am.

Neither of us backed away. All the best people are a little bit off their head, aren't they? I figured I could help her get well. Figured she could do the same for me, provided I stay worthy. I couldn't expect unconditional love, after all. I would have to provide. I would need to be strong and funny and dependable. I would need to put everybody else first. I would need to be supportive and present and true. I would take on whatever came at me. I would be all that she had fantasised about, and more. And maybe, if I exceeded myself in perpetuity, she might like me enough to let me be a wretched, pitiful bastard for a while, and wouldn't judge me too harshly for sobbing into her stomach for the few months it might take me to cry out all the toxins and bitter tears.

She rewrites our story when her mood is low, but I still feel as though I know the truth of it. We were unhappy people. She'd had a Hellish childhood. I didn't, but I'd somehow turned it into one in my own head. Neither of us expected to live as long as we had. We were a mixed bag of contradictions, neuroses and oscillating virtues. We hated ourselves and felt unappreciated. We were worthless, but entitled to more than we had. We loved our children, but resented having to stay alive just so they wouldn't be messed up by our departure. We fell in love with such ease that it truly seemed as though we were one entity that had somehow been broken apart. We each saw ourselves reflected in the other. We spoke, in those early days, about our demons playing together. We hoped to make one another happy, and at the very least, we knew we would understand and forgive one another's madness. She would be patient with my depression. I would give her the emotional support she needed to become all that she could be. The baby wasn't really planned, but we were both high on newness and each other. When Artemisia arrived, I swear I felt nothing but joy. I'd made it, in my way. A novelist. A man in love. A dad. A chance to make up for the worst mistakes of last time, and to truly prove I'd put the worst of myself away.

Post Natal Depression dragged her into places I couldn't reach. Borderline Personality Disorder. Attention Deficit Hyperactivity Disorder. Suicidal ideation. Peri-Menopause. The last few years have been breakdowns and explosions and bouts of apocalyptic wretchedness and rage. She loathes herself more than any person I've ever known. I try to see out though her eyes and it half kills me to see the pain that lives within her. All the bad things that happen are her fault, you see. She's worthless. Repulsive. Bad. The good things that happen would have been ever better if not for her. She's destroyed so many lives that she deserves nothing but continual misery and if she allows herself to think positively about the future, terrible things will happen. She's out of control. She doesn't trust herself, or me. She doesn't deserve happiness or good times. She's repackaged me as a symptom of her mental illness. I'm just the latest in a long line of impulsive, self-destructive decisions. She's toxic. Being with her has destroyed my career. Loving her has turned me into everything that I hate and I'd be better off with somebody else, anybody else: I should just let her go and take our daughter and let her own children go back to the ex she thinks of as one of the worst people in the world. Everything would be better if she were just, please, allowed to die.

But Kathleen's getting through to her, I think. She's able to talk about things like we used to. She can take a joke again. Her temper isn't so close to the surface. She smiles when she wakes up sometimes. She stretches like a cat waking up in a square of sunlight.

She does it now. Stretches and sits up and takes my hand when I put it down next to hers.

We talk for a while. Kathleen wants her to fill in a form about aspects of her mental health. She's cross with herself for not having done it yet so we sit in bed and cuddle and she reads out some of the questions on the form. We have to tick the ones that apply to us?

- I find it hard to be kind to myself
- If something goes wrong I automatically blame myself
- I don't deserve to do nice things for myself
- I am very critical of myself when things aren't going well
- I am very critical of myself even when things are going well
- When I am having a hard time, I wouldn't even think to look after myself like I would a friend
- I focus a lot on my faults and flaws and can't let them go
- If I make a mistake I give myself a really hard time
- When I am struggling, I don't treat myself with much care
- If I make a mistake I feel like I should be punished I feel like I'm the only one who struggles or fails at things…

More ticks than a Swiss watch factory. I hate being so bloody textbook.

Familiar feelings begin to prickle and press within my skin. I see the same lumpen mass of fibre-glass and papier Mache that used to swim in my vision when I looked into my deepest recessed and tried to decide what I really felt about things.

Soon, we're talking about Mam. It comes to Mam more often than seems fair. I realise how petty my resentments sound. I get ratty. I mention the notion of 'unconditional love' and get pissed off with myself as soon as I subject my thoughts to any kind of analysis. Love should be conditional, shouldn't it? Isn't that the point of setting boundaries? Isn't that what we're supposed to do to safeguard ourselves from the excesses of those around us? Doesn't unconditional love simply give somebody a licence to be dreadful? I start to feel tired as I talk about it and I don't really want answers or input so I drop the whole thing and talk about Dad instead. Doesn't seem fair, I say. He was the manic depressive and yet he was the fun one. He'd play football. We'd build shelters in the woods. He took me golfing in a downpour. We'd chat about football and wrestlers and who would win in a fight between Stuart Pearce and Mr T…

I talk for ages. This was supposed to be about her and here we are, again, stirring the mulch inside my head and seeing what rises to the surface. Always the same, more or less. Same problems now as then.

I'm objectionable. What I put out to the world – I'm funny, irreverent, charming, weird… they're the things people admire when they see them in a celebrity. Comedians, pop stars, actors – they pop on TV and say funny, naughty things and everybody thinks they're great. But when it's me, I get in trouble. I get criticized. I get steered away from being me, to being somebody less objectionable, less hard to like. 12-tears-old and I'm already aware that there's something about me that rubs people up the wrong way. So I compensate. I try harder to get a laugh or a reaction. And every time it works I feel a little bit less terrible about myself. And then I get in trouble for it. For being arrogant or scornful or big-headed, and all I'm doing is repeating jokes that everybody howled at when Billy Connolly and Ben Elton said them, and ….

And I have to go to pick up the littlest from nursery. I can't be late again. Three days ago I was told that my lateness simply wasn't acceptable. I was 12 minutes late because they'd closed the road and I'd had to take the eldest to his driving lesson in Hexham. I'd done everything in my power to meet my commitments. Tick the boxes. Be what everybody wanted. Not good enough. Never good enough.

And I sit here not knowing if I'm sinking into a depression or feeling sorry for myself. Self love can't be unconditional, can it? That would be obscene.

13

Somebody To Love

I'm in the thick of the madness when we meet. Drowning in it. Drowning in my own sick self. Fist down my throat and that ever-present ringing in my ears. Drowning, while everybody else paddles in the shallows and takes their big, cleansing breaths.

Carlisle's a small place, so I have no doubt that everybody knows who I am and what a disaster I'm making of my life. I feel like I'm wrapped in a big damp banner with the words 'cunt' and 'loser' and 'still better than you' written on it every shade of red and black and sadness. I'm getting it all wrong. Wasting my potential. Fucking it up. Fading. Becoming less, even as I strive for more. I want to hurt. I want to be hurt. I want more pain, and less.

I've been given a permanent junior reporter position at the newspaper but I haven't had anybody to tell or to celebrate with, so it's morphed into a reason to feel dreadful rather than proud of myself. My ex has got somebody new; somebody easier to deal with. I'm still living at home. Mam and Dad look at each other with knowing eyes every time I open my mouth. The band is over, and my attempts to start a new one have been hampered by the fact I'm so shit a guitarist that I can't play my own songs. More than that, and there have been a couple of complaints on the letters page pointing out errors in my reviews of gigs and movies. I can't function without my rituals. I keep losing chunks of time. I've stopped wearing my glasses in the hope that the hallucinations become as blurry as everything else. It doesn't work. They're still crystal clear and I spend my life squinting just to see where I'm going and giving myself headaches that seem to drill through my jawbone and into the noxious pulp of my brain.

I'm still doing what I have to, though. There's no medals for that. Nobody appreciates the fact that I'm absolutely, steadfastly refusing to open my veins. And I'm still moving forward. I can just about find the strength to go to work, though I spend great chunks of time sitting in the toilet stalls and reading then re-reading the same extract of American poetry that seems to soothe me if I look at it enough times while copying it out onto my thigh with my fingertip. I've dyed the tips of my hair purple so that people realise I'm not like them, and I keep seeing people with other peculiar affectations with which to mark themselves out and which make mine seem terribly weak by comparison.

I'm drinking, too. I don't have much money to spend on my nights out but having a column on club life in the local newspaper means that the owners are pretty good at keeping my glass filled. I've got a taste for Newcastle Brown, but whisky is starting to slip, insidiously, into my thoughts. I'm not smoking weed regularly yet. I don't know what it will do to me and I'm not yet sufficiently full of self-loathing to find out.

I recognize her from previous nights out in this, Carlisle's token 'alternative' nightclub. It's 1996. Summer. And I'm in one of the few indoor spaces where I feel comfortable. I used to come here with the girlfriend who broke my heart but I'm not about to stop visiting just because it has painful associations. Moreover, there's nowhere else to go. I'm black clothes and cord bracelets, Celtic jewelry and plectrums in my pocket. I like songs that thud and crash and fill my head with sound and feeling. I need my music to have a drummer and a vocalist and a beat that makes my spine shake. I need this place. Here, it's Nirvana and Reef, Marilyn Manson and Korn. I feel the worst parts of myself retreat when I'm thrashing my head around to Rage against the Machine. There's a peace to be found in this sweat and beer, this eye-liner and leather' this smoke and grease and press of flesh.

She's spreadeagled at the bottom of the stairs, merrily drunk. The double doors keep swinging open and people are stepping over her on their way to the dancefloor. Her dress, cut to an inch below her bum, has snagged the heel of her Doc Marten and she's got herself tied up: all twisted and tangled and finding it rather funny. Her hair has been shaved around the back and sides and what's left has been split down the middle and tied in bunches. She's got big eye and a big smile. She's 18, and she's ben going to clubs for a couple of years already. She's got three mates who look like her. Me and the ex used to call them The Craft, after the Goth-friendly movie., I know she wears a long dark coat and fish-nets, a bobble hat and fingerless gloves. She looks like the most cheerful out of her gang. They drift through the city centre in a mass of black but she's always got a smile on her face and finding something to chuckle at.

I notice that she's showing off more of herself than she would wish to in sobriety. People hang about on the stairs so they can hear one another talk and most are throwing the odd glimpse in the direction of her gusset, which strikes me as somewhat ungentlemanly. So I bend down and sit her up a little straighter and pull her skirt down, and she giggles, because apparently I've told her she "should probably cover her dignity". I may have added a 'darling' on the end. I'm giving out 'darlings' like sweeties at the time. 'Giving out 'mate' and 'laddo' and 'captain' to the lads. I've got a Geordie twang in my accent so I can manage a 'sweetheart' and 'pet' without sounding too much of an arsehole. That's what I tell myself, at least.

We kiss the next time we see each other. I'm sitting on a step facing the dancefloor, watching people bounce off one another in the smoke and the darkness. I'm holding my forefinger and thumb up to my face; the digits half an inch apart, as if I'm inspecting a fine jewel. I'm on my own. I usually am. It's years before I realise that nobody's ever invited me to meet for a drink beforehand or come in with them. I've attached myself to a gang of best friends and it doesn't occur to me that I might be a nuisance. I'm a journalist on the local paper. I was in a band that everybody loved. I've got good anecdotes and I'm funny. Even the voices in my head don't think to tell me that I haven't actually got any friends.

"Are you crushing people's heads?"

She squats down in front of me. Cigarette breath, fruity perfume, body spray, toothpaste and Jack Daniel's.

"I am," I say, and it doesn't feel odd to admit it. Yeah, of course I'm crushing people's heads. I'm squishing them like brambles. And through the filter of my madness, I can really see the gore.

"I do that," she says, brightly. "My friends think I'm weird."

She kisses me, or I kiss her, and it's warm and wet and nice. I find myself smiling. She smiles too, within the kiss. "I've got to find my friends," she says, as we part. And she squeezes my hand, which has found hers during the embrace. I remember that squeeze on the walk home. I can still taste her on my top lip but it's the hand-squeeze I can't shake. There's something tender within it. Something that speaks of boundless compassion and a great internal reservoir of empathy, sympathy, patience. For the duration of the walk home, I'm not mad. I'm not depressed. I'm lovestruck; high.

I'm at work for 8am. Dad drops me off. I've got a few bits and bobs to deal with in the main office and then I'm back up to the city centre after lunch. I spend the morning thinking of the girl. I remember that I've kissed her friend. I remember making a joke at her expense with my last girlfriend. I remember the feel of her hand: the fine framework of her fingers, the cool of her palm. I think about all the times I've seen her and her friends ambling through the city centre in their big black coats. I wonder whether she might be around today.

I'm in the main shopping street when I see her and her best friend. She's dressed not unlike she was last night. She looks shocked and pleased when I walk up to her. I ask her out for a drink and she flicks her gaze in the direction of her friend, presuming the question is being asked of her. It's not awkward. I'm okay at things like this. I've been a journalist for about a year-and-a-half and I don't worry about making a prat of myself. I'm good with words and eye contact doesn't concern me. So she laughs and says yes, if her friend doesn't mind, and we go for a drink in The Boardroom, where the landlord knows me and can be relied upon to talk to me as if I'm a bigshot rather than a cock.

She drinks neat bourbon. She tells me she's 18 and she's waiting for her A- level results and wants to be an archaeologist. I ask her if she would like to go out for a nice meal and she's surprised, but seems happy. We got for dinner the same night: Carlisle's only French restaurant. I don't eat much, but I don't puke before we meet, and I take that as a positive sign. She's impressed when I order the 'house red'. We go to the park afterwards and sit by the river and she's so nervous when we kiss that one of her hands goes oddly numb and then she has a bit of a panic attack and tells me she's afraid of the dark.

I don't tell her about the demons or the voices and I play down the sadness. I big myself up. I've got plans. I'm going to be a journalist for a while but I really want to be an author. I write poems and little snippets of this and that. She tells me she loves reading. Loves Star Trek and nature documentaries and metal music. She wants to get an eyebrow piercing. Her dad used to be Mayor. She's only slept with one person. She was bullied at school. She's a redhead, under the dye. She gave a bouquet of flowers to Princess Diana when she was a little girl. And yes, she's been thinking about me. She's going to university in a few weeks, but that doesn't seem to matter. I feel good, and I seem to be making her feel good too. I like holding her hand. I like how she listens. She's funny. Clever. Sweet.

We marry when I'm 22 and she's 20. Too young, of course, but I think it will help me commit to living, and it will make her smile in that bright-eyed way of hers. I don't cheat for ages. But when I do, I feel no guilt. I'm miserable. Failing at everything. Becoming so intolerably beige that I sometimes think about killing somebody just to give the day a bit of excitement. In the absence of that, maybe punching somebody or robbing somebody or seducing somebody will make me feel briefly like less of a loser. I'm searching for unequivocal highs. I'm desperate to feel the satisfaction of putting somebody on their arse or making some big lad's neglected wife cross her eyes and curl her toes with pleasure. I'm full of hate and sadness and the alternative is to go to bed and pull the covers over my head and sink into the cotton and springs. So I tell myself it's okay. But it's not. And I don't feel any better. I can write, though. I can find more black bile and fetid blood within my veins than ever before. So I write it. Write me. Write the worst of myself. She reads it, likes it, loves it. Tells me this could really be something. I'm too arrogant and wretched and caught up in myself to hear her when she warns that people will hate the main character: the alcoholic, womanizing journalist. He's abhorrent. A grotesque. He's clearly mad. Clearly dangerous.

I'm so high on the whole thing that I feel the overwhelming urge to do something celebratory. Something significant.

I'm not allowed to kill myself now. I'm writing something good.

So I do the next best thing.

I suggest we have a baby.

14.

Nasty, Brutish and Short

I'm 5ft 8". It's the tallest I've ever been. It's the tallest I'll ever be, barring some horrific bungee accident or a comedy pratfall in front of a steamroller.

I'm very much aware that this is not remotely tall enough. The rules were made very clear when I was still little (ha!) and my teenage years confirmed it. If you're a lad who wears glasses, plays woodwind and carries a comb in their back pocket, you damn well better be 6ft 5".

I'm telling this because it's come up as an issue in several relationships, and has been mentioned in a few counselling sessions as well. I have 'Little Man Syndrome'. I have a 'Napoleon Complex'. It work so hard to be remembered as a six-footer that it virtually dictates my every action in new company. I exhibit both sides of my personality as quickly as I can when making a new acquaintance. I'll show what's good about me. I'm a writer. I'm a good dad. I'm physically pretty strong. I'm determined. I'm poetic. I'm kind. I'm resourceful. I'll do whatever it takes for those I love. I'll put myself last.

I have to compensate, you see. My personality and my achievements have to add inches. I have to be able to drink until there's nothing left and still be able to recite Dylan Thomas. I have to be the shoulder to cry on for the neglected wives of the big, tough men who don't know that their partner needs poetry and tenderness and a bit of damned attention. I have to stand nose-to-chest with the hardest guy in the pub and tell him that he's taken my turn at the bar. I need to be the guy who'll do what others are afraid to do. I have to be remarkable. I have to be more than I appear to be. I have to disguise the fact I'm a little bloke, with a gut and no hair and a tendency to get an upset stomach in times of particular stress.

Part of my depression? A strand of my mental illness? I don't know. But I've shed more tears about my fear of not measuring up than I have about anything else. I don't know how to disentangle my sense of worth from all the adolescent abuse I received for being, well, me.

I only recently discovered that being short isn't something to feel bad about. Neither is being overweight, or needing spectacles, or suffering acne or being crap at football. This all seems a little counter-intuitive to me, as in my experience, every step you are away from the perceived ideal, is a step further away from perfection. And if you move far enough away from perfection, you reach 'imperfect'. And from there, the scale slides down and down. And if being short and fat and bespectacled isn't something to make fun of, why do people make fun of it? Why does every bloody participant on First Dates tell the host that they're hoping to meet somebody who's "tall, obviously".

Forgive me if this becomes more about venting spleen than it does delving into my depression, but I think there may be a bit of overlap.

School is hard for everybody. People had it worse than me. My best friend at school was a teacher's son. He had more money than the rest of us, had a nose so crooked that it appeared to have an elbow, and he had a Welsh name. At a school that only cared about football, he played rugby. He rode horses, visited the South of France and sometimes came into school wearing non-uniform as he was leaving at lunchtime to compete in something called modern-pentathlon. His life between 9 and 4 was absolutely bloody torture. But he was a big lad. He was tough. He fought back. He didn't worry about getting hurt and he knew that taking a punch really wasn't that big a deal. He'd get upset now and again but he had a mate in me who was very good at dishing out insults that cut to the bone, and then standing behind him.

I couldn't do what he did. I was small. I was slightly built. I seemed to annoy people on sight. I didn't have the right trainers. We didn't have a car. I loved football but wasn't any good at it. I wouldn't play-fight. I thought farts were uncouth. I told girls they looked en-chanting. I played the clarinet and saxophone and sometimes had to stand up in front of the year-group and read out a poem I'd written. I talked to the teachers about authors and composers. I listened to jazz and classical music. I took pride in my hair and didn't like it being messed up. I really, really liked the softness and scent of female skin.

I couldn't have been more of a target for abuse if I'd gone to school wearing my nana's nightdress.

I learned how to compensate: how to deflect. I took what I'd learned in fiction and started exhibiting the characteristics of the heroes, and protagonists to whom readers had undoubtedly warmed. I started being funny. I learned whole routines by Billy Connolly, Bill Hicks, Jack Dee, Richard Pryor and use their timing and their material in a bid to get the bullies to move on. I'd be kind, as opportunity arose. I'd give my friends clever one-liners to say if they were getting picked on. I got very good at the saxophone and okay on the guitar. I said naughty things to teachers and got big laughs in return. I became somebody that people talked to about their problems. I did the occasional piece of homework for people in distress. I ended relationships on behalf of people who were too awkward to tell their boyfriend or girlfriend that it was over. I wrote music for the school plays and made sure people knew that I was a bit of a ladies' man. I wore a leather jacket to school.

I got it all wrong, of course. In reality, Goliath kicks the shit out of David. In actuality, Poirot gets his moustache rubbed in the dirt and Oliver Twist ends up dying of consumption at 15. The things that impressed me had the opposite effect on the mouth-breathing slabs of pigflesh that made my life miserable. Now, because of the amount of time I spent with 'the lasses', I was obviously gay. Playing music and writing poems marked me out as 'a proper fanny'. Dark hair and dusky skin meant I was foreign, so I took a few years of racial abuse: a proxy for the absent ethnicities. I spent half my life in a headlock or nursing dead arms and dead legs. I had my bike stolen, my watch stolen. I was forced to say things to people that were guaranteed to get me a beating and provoke hearty laughs among one group of tormentors as they served me up to another. All the while I thought of the future. All the while I fixated on that day, a few years down the line, when they'd be staring out the window of the Job Centre, sallow-faced and dead-eyed, and see me drive past in a convertible on my way to launch my latest novel. I'd still be short, but my aura would have a surfeit of added inches.

I was in my late teens and sinking into my own private realm of anguish and misery when I stopped allowing other people to dictate how much suffering I was going to endure. I started standing up for myself. Started hitting back. Became a scrappy little nutter who wasn't worth the bother. I've carried that on into adulthood. I've worked the doors on city centre pubs. I've stood my ground in front of lads who've wanted to tear me to shreds. I've interviewed psychopaths and serial killers and walked waded into crowds of braying rioters to find somebody willing to give a quote to the local newspaper. I've always been scared but I've faced my fears so often that I know how to safely ignore all those warning voices telling me something is a really bad idea. I've learned how to hide my cowardice. I'm not somebody who gets bullied. I'm not somebody who lets fear win.

Does any of this affect my mental health? Is my personality a direct result of being the kid who wasn't allowed outside on sunny days in case their hay-fever flared up? Have I fought and cheated and done all that I've done as a direct consequence of being picked on for being little and weird? I don't bloody know. But there's no doubt we live in a society that still views people by their appearance, and that men are meant to be big and strong. Tall, dark and handsome would be ideal. I do know that I write books about a character who's 6ft 6" and hugely muscled. He's gentle. He loves his wife and family. He's shy and doesn't feel the need to put himself forward. He blushes if he makes a fool of himself.

Interviewers ask where he comes from when he's so different from me. And I don't know if they're joking. He's just who I'd be if I was big. Everything about me would be different if I were big. But I'm not, except around the middle, and that, apparently, doesn't count.

But I'm cool with it. Honest.

15

Ritual Sacrifice and The Stairs in TopShop

There are three sections to the stairs in TopShop in Carlisle. To ensure you reach the top step of each section with your left foot leading, you need to start the first section with your left foot, the second little dog-leg with your right, and then the final bit with your left. While doing this you must also listen to the voice in your head saying "left, right, left" in the accent of an American drill sergeant.

You are permitted two circuits of the store. On the first pass you must pick up three items, look at the price, stroke the front and then replace them at the back of the rail. During the second circuit you must replace them in their original position. In your pocket, you must write out the words "All ways and always" on your leg using your fingertip as a pencil. Your pockets will, of course, be full of the bus tickets, receipts and chewing gum wrappers that have been with you during previous positive experiences so that they can, in some sense, continue to imbue you with their powers. If you complete these rituals without deviation, you'll become a novelist, you'll find love with an artist who adores you and your grandparents will live until they are in their eighties.

I know all this because I have Obsessive Compulsive Disorder. I don't have it the way I used to but it's still there. I need to brush my teeth in a certain way and there is a complex routine involving tap rotation that I won't bore you with, but I don't collapse in on myself in fits of absolute panic when I fail to carry out one of my rituals correctly.

A lot of people think that OCD means liking things neat; liking things ordered, or 'just-so'. It's not like that for me. Mine is more like an obsessive religion – a fanatical belief in a personal religion which has its own ever-changing rituals and dogma. It's superstition taken to the extreme. It's a means of feeling in control while your life disintegrates around you. At 18 I had no doubt that I had unlocked the secret of the universe. All I had to do to guarantee perpetual happiness was perform the exact same thing I had done on a previous occasion when things had gone well. I needed to see the same faces, have the same conversations, visit the same stores, wave to the same cars. I had to take the same route; tie my shoes at the same spot – make the same exclamations as I had the last time, and things would go well for me. Nobody would laugh at me, my girlfriend would be in a good mood, I'd do something well at work and I'd write a poem of actual worth. It escalated quickly, of course. Life doesn't permit endless repetition so there had to be forfeits and sacrifice. If I was unable to wear the same clothes I'd have to at least carry the same rubbish in my pockets. If I didn't see the same car as I had the day before then I needed to put a cross on the heel of my shoe to counter-act the failure. If I reached the top of a flight of stairs with my right foot leading I would have to scurry down to the bottom and start again to ensure my left foot was leading when I reached the top. If in company I could forestall the act of penitence, provided I return to the staircase at the first available opportunity and carry out the act three times.

The writing on my leg was the most debilitating. I learned short-hand at 17 and got into the habit of writing down everything everybody said; my finger twitching across my leg like a caterpillar on a hot-plate. I was hearing voices at the time so I'd write that down too. And then I'd remember that I believed in God, and They didn't care much for my worship of these false idols, so I should write down a line of scripture instead so that god knew I was doing this to praise Him rather than spite Him, but the voices would whisper blasphemies and I'd find myself scribbling down lines of putrid, sacrilegious profanity. The only possible repentance was through pain and suffering. So wouldn't eat, or I'd deny myself acts of pleasure, or I'd start a fight with some-body I cared about so as to get my punishment out of the way early.

By 19, I knew that the only way I would get to live the kind of life that mattered to me was by fully embracing the code onto which I had stumbled. I had to read and re-read every love letter I'd ever been sent before leaving the house. I had to put on yesterday's socks, remove them and then rub them against today's socks before putting them on, taking them off and swapping feet. I had to rub the bedstead in a certain way before leaving my room. The light switch needed to be flicked off, then on, then off and on again and I had to leave without looking back to see whether the room was illumi-nated or in darkness. And the day went downhill from there. It was torture and I looked properly mad. I was very close to becoming one of those local characters who mutter to themselves and poison their neighbours' milk. But it was for a purpose. It was a pre-emptive penance. This was what was required of me in order to become a successful novelist; to know true love, and to keep my grandparents alive until I was ready to lose them. And it was a small price to pay.

Did it stop? When? How? I told my teenage shrink all about it and he was kind enough to fill my head with new words. Obsessive Compulsive Disorder. I read the pamphlets. I recognised the symptoms. I read a case study about somebody in America with exactly the same rituals as me who was living in a mental hospital and had no skin on her hands because she believed that peeling off her flesh and eating it would stop people from leaving her. It didn't sound as though it was working, and if her's was an illness then maybe mine was too. So, on balance, it was probably worth stopping the rituals. Stopping the rituals became a ritual in itself. I had to complete several weeks of doing the inverse of everything I'd done previously, so as to somehow demonstrate a willingness to reset my metaphysical hourglass to its original position.

My grandparents all died in their eighties. I'm a novelist, and I've known true love.

If I'd kept up the rituals another week longer, perhaps I'd have made less of a balls up of everything that's happened since.

16

Sick Of It

I'm on my knees again. This is where I make my devotions – where my prayers are most fervent; here, retching and jerking and puking up yellow bile onto my own hazy reflection.

I'm 18 now. I've been puking for years. It helps me feel a little better. It's impossible to throw up when there's nothing in your body so I've started purging myself before every activity to ensure there can be no embarrassments. It's my way of being in control. I throw up every day, even when my body doesn't want to. I don't have to suffer the indignity of sticking my fingers down my throat – I just think about myself and my pitifulness and my rank, abject weakness, and my gut contracts and I emit violent streams of watery acid. I puke until I'm empty. It makes the blood vessels pop in my forehead and in my eyes, but I wear sunglasses most of the time and haven't shaved my head yet, so nobody sees unless they look really closely.

People hear, of course. I'm working as a junior reporter at the news and Star and my office is in the city centre. I have a key and the pass-code, which means I can pop in of an evening to throw my guts up without fear of interruption. Pub toilets are good for this too. Nobody bats an eye at the sound of fevered vomiting from behind the cubicle door. People sometimes shout encouragement.

It's at home that I struggle. Mam can hear a mouse trip over a pebble in the back garden and she gets up to pee 14 times a night, so I have to learn to puke without making a sound. I get good at throwing up at the exact moment I flush the toilet so that the sound is obscured. Even so, she finds out. I don't tell anybody but somehow she gets wise to the way I've chosen to handle things. She understands. She gets anxious too. She gets an upset stomach when she's nervous about things. She can't keep weight on and is extremely fragile, like a porcelain doll wrapped in calfskin. She tells me that Paul McCartney is always physically sick before he goes on stage, and I take some kind of comfort from knowing I'm not alone. But I can't ask the questions I want to ask. Does he also throw up before he sees his girlfriend?

Does he throw up when he catches sight of himself in the darkened screen of the computer? Does he vomit when he realise he's going to have to spend several awkward hours in a car with somebody else?

Right now, I'm on my knees and throwing up harder than I ever have. I'm meeting my girlfriend, the love of my life, in about half an hour. She wants to do it outdoors. It's a fantasy and I know a place. She's very excited. I've got to make sure the experience lives up to the dream. The pressure makes me feel nauseous, which means I need to puke. And so I'm puking so hard that there are little red fireflies dancing in my eyes and the tendons in my neck are sticking out like the bars of a birdcage. I'm punching the wall with the back of my hand, furious and disgusted and utterly engorged with self-loathing. My jaw pops out of the socket. I taste blood. I can't breathe suddenly and my spare hand is clawing at my throat where the usual acid fire is replaced with a ball of hot gristle. My fingers tangle in my necklace. It's a leather cord from which dangle two pendants. On one, the word 'joyful' is picked out in silver lettering. The other reads 'secure'. They were presents from my girlfriend, to help me feel better about myself. She's read my poems. My letters. She's seen what's underneath the veneer. She wants me to feel good. I deserve to feel good, apparently. She says this like it's some unequivocal truth – that people should be kind to themselves and generally forgive the parts of their personality that they don't particularly like. But she cries about her weight and her hair and she used to cut herself with razors and she thinks she's a rubbish artist in the face of all evidence to the contrary. She's aloof and scornful with me and sometimes she says we won't necessarily be together forever and that she wants to properly live the university experience when she goes, and despairs of me when I go quiet or sad or tell her about some other girl at work who's taken a shine to me. When I repeat her advice back to her she tells me that self-doubt is normal, but self-loathing to the point of suicidal ideation is an illness that needs to be treated. And I tell her I don't need treatment, I just need her to be nicer to me.

Twenty-five years later and I'm on my knees in the downstairs bathroom. Puking, as per usual. I use the bathroom furthest away from everybody else. The kids don't particularly like the sound of me being violently sick so I'm content to take myself away to indulge in my private little ritual. I still try and muffle it with towels and running taps. It's not far off midnight but no doubt one of them is still awake and watching some mind-numbing shit on their phone and the last thing I need is to think of them sending their friends WhatsApp messages explaining that their joke of a dad is busy throwing up his own spleen because he's realized, again, how pitiful he is.

I managed twenty minutes of sleep before the tickle woke me up. It's a feather; a petal, a flake of por-pourri; a dreadful acid prickle at that little place between the throat and the lungs. I have gastro-esophageal reflux disorder, now. I have a hiatus hernia. There's a big gap at the top of my stomach which means that my food flows back up my throat if I lay down or move too quickly in the hour or two after eating. I can't handle spicy food. I don't tend to vomit with anxiety as much as I did but the damage that I did during those many years of violent regurgitation has torn my insides to shreds. So too has the whisky. My insides are a mess. Stomach acid has turned my tongue a funny colour and dissolved the enamel on my back teeth. My jaw dislocates a couple of times a day and doesn't always go back in. My gag reflex kicks in if I put an ice lolly a millimeter too far down my throat. Sometimes I'm so dehydrated that the migraines arrive in a perfect punch to the forehead, putting me down to my knees and shoving its greasy thumbs into my eyes. Then I can't work, which makes me anxious …

I've talked about all this with my shrinks over the years. The good one, the one I paid for, spoke with something akin to awe at the way I had seemingly separated my mind from my physical body. I was punishing the vessel into which my consciousness had been poured – allowing me the confidence to be and do and say whatever the day required. I felt rather proud of that. One of my GPs was less encouraging. He told me I really had to stop being sick or I was going to do myself untold damage. The anti-nausea pills he gave me were very powerful. It took a huge effort for my body to throw them up, but we managed in the end. Sobriety didn't help either. The alcohol was a big help in masking my insecurities, though too much of it did tend to make me throw up my anti-depressants and my gastric reflux medication.

It comes as a shock to people when I tell them how nervous nausea has devastated huge tracts of my life. I always seem so confident, apparently. I'm self-assured. I'm the life of the party. I don't seem to have a nervous bone in my body. I always feel intense delight at having fooled people. Of course I seem that way – I've taken care of business. I can't throw up, there's nothing in me. I can get on. I can make you laugh or make you think or say something flirty and see where it leads. I can hold court in a packed bar and I can face down a bailiff on the doorstep or a boisterous dad at a soft play centre and nobody will ever know that my insides feel like water and that I'll slip away to puke out the adrenaline and fear as soon as it's all over.

One of the kids has to give a presentation at school in a week or so. She's 15 and arty and gets herself in a state about stuff. She's panicking about giving the presentation. She fears she'll burst into tears in front of the class. She wants us to write a note getting her out of it, explaining that she has a nervous condition that means she 'simply can't' undertake the task. I don't know what's best. Make her do it and give her the opportunity to realise that it's not that scary? Explain that life is full of things that we don't want to do but that growing up involves finding the inner strength to overcome them? Or should I write the note? Accept that she's terrified and that it's too much to ask her to face this particular fear I should have lots of experience to draw upon. I should have colossal reserves of empathy and be willing to do anything to spare her the absolute terror which she's enduring. Or is she just making a fuss? Is she being melodramatic? Am I minimizing her genuine feelings of acute distress? I don't know. So often I find myself torn between the theoretical and the experiential. I know that the best thing to do in all circumstances is to listen and understand and to try and navigate a path between the obstacles together. I also know that she's a teenager and bone-idle and makes very much the same amount of fuss about having to do the dishes or watch her little sister.

I try and tell her that it feels wonderful to overcome a fear. I've spent my whole adult life doing things that scare me and that's what's got me to where I am ….

She gives a dismissive wave of her hand that suggests that where I am is absolutely nowhere. It hurts all the way to the bone.

And now it's nearly midnight, and that dismissive wave has tickled my throat. I can't sleep. I'm doubting myself. Doubting my ability to provide for my family; to get back to the bestseller list – to provide a safe space for her and her siblings to realise their dreams. It's waking up the voices in my head. I'm seeing things. My guts are churning and I keep giving the little cough that means I'm fighting with my own body.

I take control. Totter to the bathroom and get down on my knees. I'll be okay. I just need to take control. I need to rid myself of the fear. I need to puke until my gums bleed and the fireflies dance.

Come tomorrow, nobody will have a clue.

17.

Guilt-Edged

"You're just like everybody else".

That was Mam's pet phrase, along with *"careful, mind"* and *"why's it always your voice I can hear above everybody else?"*. She's a kind person is Mam but she has an uncanny ability to stick a crowbar in the cracks in my armour and lever them apart. Being just like everybody else was intended to be comforting but given that I hated my life and everybody with whom I had been unfairly deposited and was being mercilessly bullied by the kind of mouth-breathing thugs who could fall into a sausage machine and come out more useful, it didn't do me any good. I wanted to be different. Special. Chosen. I wanted my suffering to be a part of my journey to somewhere remarkable. I wanted to be extraordinary so I could ram my incredible successes down the throats of everybody who had ever doubted me, picked on me, thought me too small or overlooked me in favour of some thick-necked football player with a shaved head and an ability to fart on command. I wasn't one of them. I didn't want to be thought of as different – I wanted to be recognized as superior. I wanted to be told that school was temporary and that once I got out of the wildlife documentary of my teenage years, the world would recognize me as a romantic, a poet, a musician, a true Renaissance man. It seems like she was going out of her way to be unhelpful. It was like she was describing a stranger. She'd tell me she didn't think I'd ever leave Carlisle. Tell me I was too much of a 'home bird' to ever fly the nest. I was sweet and caring and that all the stuff on the service was just bravado. By the time I left Elora and her mum, she didn't think that any more. I think she thought the bravado had devoured whatever she hoped was there underneath. When Dad told her he was leaving, she was probably right when she told him he was 'just like David'. I'm sure she thought I'd given him the idea.

I didn't help, in the aftermath. I was on Dad's side. He'd found love. He deserved happiness. He'd worked so hard to try and make her happy and she was just such a damn killjoy. Such a mood-hoover. Such a pain. I look back and I swear the only thing I can remember thinking was a perverse pleasure that, yet again, the conventional way; the path of doing things properly, had been exposed as a sham once again. I was right, again. It was all pain and suffering and unhappiness and all you could do was experience some brief moments of pleasure before the sweet release of death. I think I said this out loud in quite a few pubs. If you were there, sorry.

Mam and me didn't talk much. And when we did I was an un-speakable arsehole. She was just putting herself back together when she asked me to be honest with her and tell her the truth about why he left. What the other woman had that she didn't. I was drunk on whisky and bile. I'd spend all the money from the family house sale and quit my job in a fit of temper. I'd set up a business that nobody wanted. I'd bought a house I couldn't afford and had just successfully persuaded my ex to pay for my new partner's HGV driving course. I was seeing Elora every day but she was insanely jealous of letting other people talk to me and would grab my face and hold it next to hers so that there was only her in my world, and it all felt as though she was doing it on purpose to make me see what a stupid, wretched bastard I was for walking away. I was about a week away from what I and Arthur Fowler would recognize as a true breakdown.

I came right out and said it, plain, simple and inescapable.

"You're just a pain in the arse, Mam".

I genuinely didn't think it would cause such a rumpus. I thought that was the role she'd chosen for herself and which she'd performed with such considerable aplomb.

I think I'm well at the moment. I can steer my thoughts instead of be steered by them. I feel moments of huge joy and real contentment. Sometimes, I experience something a lot like happiness. In such moments, I can look back upon moments and decide what I feel about them without the filter of self-pity and alcohol. And I still feel bloody awful for what I said to my mam. I still wish I'd told her, instead, that I was so unhappy I couldn't breathe. I wish the mask hadn't been so damned convincing.

The breakdown didn't feel like I thought it would. I just sort of unraveled. One moment I was all hate and sadness and experiencing a whole-body fat-lip of tingling numbness. And then I didn't care about anything. I was just a barely-there wisp of consciousness, forehead pressed to the cool of the bathroom wall, muttering nonsense about being sorry, so sorry, and saying 'please' until it all went dark.

Christ how I would have loved to wallow in that warm murk of pitiable nothingness. If I'd only had the good sense to loser my mind out on the street, somebody would have taken me to hospital. They'd have performed a CT scan and seen that my brain was as perfectly split as a child's drawing of a broken heart. But I lost my mind at home, where the kids and my new partner thought I was strong and funny and invincible. So I got up. I got dressed. I carried on. I drifted. I only came to life when there was the chance of getting hurt or causing trouble. I smoke and drank and cheated and fought and not a damn bit of it touched me.

So I wrote a suicide note. I put down my feelings on paper and read it back through cigarette smoke and red-rimmed eyes. It was good. Beautiful, in a terribly bleak sort of a way. It read like the sort of thing that might be written by a character in a book. I wanted to know more about this character. I wanted to help him find his path. I wanted him to see there was hope.

So I started writing. I fictionalized myself. I turned my suicide note into a novel. It was a good novel. Brilliant, according to some of the agents who got a chance to read it a year down the line. Beautiful and hard. Bleak, but marvellously so. It's just this main character. He's just so unbelievable. So putrid in his thoughts. You're meant to root for him but he's just repulsive…

Still, you have to laugh.

18.

Do I Really Feel What I Think I Feel?

Is this depression, though? Real, capital-D '**Depression**'. That's what I ask the succession of shrinks, counsellors and doctors as they roll my brain between their palms and look for cracks. Aren't I just a bit narked about things in general? Aren't I just a bit gloomy? Don't I get sad when things are going badly and giddy with glee when life's on the up?

We don't know, they say. You tell us.

It's taken me a long time to realise that there is a difference between circumstantial gloominess, and a genuine mental health disorder. Sometimes, yes, I get blue because I don't think my dad likes me very much and my career's in the toilet and I can't afford the rent. When does that become Depression? When does a disordered mind become a true disorder?

So … I consider my episodes of fear and despair. I think upon those instances when I have felt myself coming apart and reforming a billion times a second as every cell in my body explodes and implodes in a grotesque carnage of unbearable despair. I think again upon those utter, bone-crushing bouts of lethargy when it is nothing but a hatred of being a burden that stops me from laying on the floor and sinking into the earth. Depression, when it comes, is the death of the soul. It is the removal of all hope and possibility. It is forgetting what it is to be human. It is the absence of feeling; the cessation of not only all joy, but the memory of it or the possibility of its return. It is the desperate, fevered wish to not only die, but to never have existed at all.

I don't say it like this, of course. Who can say shit like that out loud? They're just people, aren't they? Doctors and nurses and counsellors. They're people who got decent grades in their science GCSEs and spent three or four years trying to pass a course. They don't know more than they've read. And they've heard it all before. They've met worse than me. They deal with people with real problems. Real suffering. Real pain. I'm just somebody who can't work out why people don't worship them like a God and who thinks they're too important to live a conventional life.

Self loathing? How dare you.

***

So, David, I hear you've had a nervous breakdown ....

Yeah. Loads of them, if you're asking. I've had the lot. Headache, racing heart, sweating like a hippo on a treadmill, desperate glugging of alcohol and night terrors that leave you so paralysed with fright that you aren't sure if you're dead until the alarm goes off. Yeah, I've served my time. One of the buggers was even classified as a 'full-blown' mental breakdown, which, as you know, is the absolute worst kind.

Incidentally, a 'nervous breakdown' is a term that describes a period of extreme mental or emotional stress. The stress is so great that the person is unable to perform normal day-to-day activities. It's not actually a term used by clinicians. It's not a mental health condition. It doesn't have a specific set of characteristics. It's basically a phrase used to explain away all sorts of horrible things like Depression, Anxiety, Insomnia, Stress. It means the hammock in your mind is carrying the weight of a blue whale. But boy have I spent my life looking out for signs I was about to have one; had just suffered one, or was on the verge of giving one to somebody else.

The phrase 'nervous breakdown' entered my life in earnest thanks to good old EastEnders and Arthur Fowler. Lovable, slightly feckless Arthur stole the Christmas club money to pay for daughter Michelle's wedding and the pressure of it all caused his mind to unravel. I can picture him now, rocking back and forward on a beer barrel, gibbering to himself. It was an arresting image. A nervous breakdown certainly seemed like something which, on balance, a chap would do well to avoid.

Before that, 'nervous breakdown' had been one of those phrases that Mam and Dad tossed around like hoopla rings. My brother and I were, it was clear, going to give Mam a nervous breakdown if we didn't pack it in. Dad was going to have one if he kept working himself so hard. My auntie was likely to have one if she kept getting so upset about little things. I was apt to have one myself if I kept getting so intense about girls...

We used it properly, after Dad. It sounded better than 'suicide attempt'. Dad had suffered a nervous breakdown through the pressure of working so hard. He was on pills now. Getting better. Focusing on what was important. He never did go and live with his Mam and Dad, or move his stuff to the little bedsit that him and Mam didn't think my brother and me knew all about. He stayed with us. Did his degree. Moved up the ladder until he was the boss of the department where he'd started out. I was there for the ceremony when he received his Masters. He wore a mortar board and a gown and seemed embarrassed and pleased with himself all at once. He pulled a silly face in the official photo. I think I was proud of him. I think I still am. He's here, after all, and he's got kids and grandkids, a pension and a house and a woman that he loves. He's funny and he buys the best presents for my girls. He still struggles with it all though. He's secretive by nature. He disappears off on holiday to exotic places and it has to be dragged out of him that he's had a good time. He gets health scares and never tells me. I only hear third hand about things I've done or not done that might have pissed off his partner. He's not had a cross word with me since I was 17. Some things sting, though. He's been on holidays that he and I had talked about doing together. Canal-boating, with my brother. The battlefields in Belgium where his uncle died during the war. They were trips we'd long promised ourselves. He went without telling me. Went with her.

19

The Price of Help

Summer, 2008.

A Tuesday afternoon, some time after 3pm.

A small and airless room above the health centre opposite the university. My seven-year-old stepson's in the beer garden of the pub next door, drinking lemonade and making a tower out of beer mats. I'm here, with my new shrink. Fifty quid an hour and if I don't get my money's worth I'll have nobody to blame but myself. .

I'm too hot. Irritable. Trying far too hard. My left leg is jiggling up and down. She notices, but I don't stop jiggling it, just so she doesn't read anything into my decision to stop.

She catches my eye.

Smiles.

I stop jiggling my leg. Hold the handle of the chair as if it were the bowl of a whisky glass. A fresh bead of sweat runs down the back of my shirt collar. It's too hot in here. The walls, with their elastoplast coloured wallpaper, seem to be perspiring, and the painted-shut windows are misting up.

She's talking again.

"I have apologised, haven't I? About the room? I tried to get another one but there's nothing available. I think if we gave that window a good shove we could get it open but then you have the sound of the road to contend with."

I tell her not to worry. I always tell people not to worry. I've got issues with other people's dissatisfaction. I don't want people feeling uncomfortable – least of all on my account. And I was already hot and sweaty and stinking of damp corduroy and dry white wine long before I walked through the door. It's hot and damp and feverish. It feels as though a great wet dog has been laying on the city: a heat-wave that has brought no blue skies. Hull sweats beneath Heavens the colour of damp concrete. It's a feverish heat; a pestilent, buzzing cloak. Even walking a few steps feels like fighting through laundry lines of damp linen. Everybody agrees that the city needs a good storm to clear the air, but, lightning has yet to split the sky.

"I thought you had enjoyed the last session. You seemed to warm up as we went along." She looks at her notes. "We were talking about your father …"

I can't seem to fool this one. She's really listening. She really seems to care. But the fifty quid is a barrier between us. Will she simply stop giving a shit when the clock hits the hour, depositing me back onto the street missing all my protective layers and vulnerable to attack?

I stare out longingly at the window. The scene it frames could be a photograph. The leaves and branches of the rowan tree are lifeless, unmoving; blocking out the view of the university across the busy.

"I feel like I'm in marriage guidance but I'm the only one here. I'm unhappy. I'm angry all the time. Nothing's going the way it was meant to. I've got things in my life that make me smile and I know I'm not allowed to kill myself but it's just all so relentless. Nobody seems to understand how hard I'm trying, but that's because I don't let them see. They should see anyway though, shouldn't they? If they love me they should be able to see past the mask. Nobody seems to have any patience with me. If somebody else is clearly feeling awful I'll ask and ask and until they give in and tell me what's really wrong. People ask me once and then believe me when I say nothing, or they lose their temper and act like I'm being a baby. They really say that! I'm being a baby!"

The psychologist puts her head on one side, like a Labrador delicately broaching the subject of a walk.

"By 'they', who do you mean?"

I stare out of the window again. I know who I mean. My partner isn't a tender person. That was what I liked about her at first. She was tough. Straightforward. She said what was on her mind. She wasn't scared of anybody. It was attractive, I think. Different, certainly. She was older than me and had a kind of refreshingly no-nonsense approach to our relationship. She drank like me. Seemed to think like me. It was only a few months in that we saw the vulnerabilities beneath one another's surface and by then my daughter was calling her "Mummy number two" and her son was calling me Dad. I want her to be gentle with me and she wants me to be strong for her. Or perhaps it's the other way around. We should never have thought we could find what we were missing in one another, but we've ourselves into our new lives as if our coupling was somehow pre-destined. It works, when we're in the pub or at a nice restaurant, seeing a movie or enjoy a day out. But we can't do reality. We're both too sensitive. She's full of rage and I sink into despair. I want to get things right; want to make sure everything I've altered about my life has been for something. So I'm in therapy, alone, talking about how I can be better. Years later, she'll call therapy 'mumbo jumbo' and I'll know that I've given 12 years to something that was never, ever meant to be more than a fleeting friendship. And for that, I'll feel so irredeemably guilty that I won't be able to think of her or see her name written down or catch a scent on the air that reminds me of her, without suffering a panic attack that puts me on my knees.

"What is it you would like the people who love you to actually say when you're in one of your depressions, David?"

I drop my head and stare at the carpet for a moment. I'm bone tired. The hot weather has made Elora irritable and she is refusing to sleep anywhere other than on Daddy.

"The things I say to them," I mutter. "I mean, they might be platitudes but they're good platitudes. I tell her she's wonderful; beautiful, sexy, clever, kind. I say a million things a day to make her feel good about herself. Nobody says anything to me and if they do it's with this grimace or this glibness that just spoils it, and I hate myself for wanting it and it's not her fault that she thinks I'm somebody else, but I'm staying alive for them, and I know I can't be happy…I accepted that, but the effort must mean something, mustn't it? seeing people try for me, like I try for them, and even if it's not real I'd appreciate the lie …,"

I stop. Listen to myself. Shake my head, exhausted with it all. I've shown her too much of myself. This is me. Nothing is ever about what it's about. Everything is bigger and grander; symbolic and representative.

"I've got an agent," I say, quietly. "Sort of. I've finished the book and he picked the manuscript out of the slush pile and really liked it. Said it was the darkest thing he'd ever read but that it's really really good. He's got me making changes. It's the character that's the problem. He's obnoxious. Repulsive. Horrible."

I look up. She's staring at me in that warm, friendly way that I need to see 24/7 from the people who are meant to like me. I want to let her help me. I like her. She's gentle and insightful and real. Admittedly, we got off to an inauspicious start. I spotted her outside the university, embroiled in a minor incident of cycle rage. It's hard to believe in somebody's power to heal your soul when you have seen them pedalling furiously down a bus lane and screaming obscenities at a Volvo.

"The character is you, yes?"

I shrug. "Bits of me. The worst of me. The best of me."

"Maybe you could write another character who has all the other bits," she says. "Somebody kind, who loves their family."

"Kind? I'm repugnant."

"Your eyes light up when you talk about your little girl. You talk about your family with real love. You're not worthless, David. Look where you are. Look what you're doing to try and be the best husband and father you can be."

"I left my wife," I say. "I left my daughter. I felt entitled to more than I was being given. I felt as though I was going to lose my mind – that I might hurt them, or hurt myself. I didn't know what I wanted but it wasn't what I had. And the next thing I was living with somebody else and had an extra kid and people were treating me with this weird kind of respect just because I was sleeping with the landlady of the pub and I hate myself so much for liking that adulation, and I played up to it. All the things my mam thinks is gross about me – they get laughs and pats on the back in the pub. In that environment I'm not a bad guy, not really, I'm just somebody who got their priorities mixed up and is doing what they can to put it right. That's better, but I don't deserve the comfort of that, so I stay at home and drink, but then I fall into my own head and the next thing it's all just so dark that I can't breathe …,"

You've never tried to end the relationship" she asks, softly.

I don't answer. I know what she'll read into it. Yes, I came damn close to walking away. We'd only been together a few weeks. She'd opened up to me. Told me about the debts and the insecurities and the bad people who were trying to take the pub off her. She'd broken down even as I started to tell her that I wasn't sure what I wanted. It was 2am and we were standing by the water's edge, both drunk on our own misery. I'd never seen anybody look so damnably unhappy. Then she pushed past me and scrambled up the railings and launched herself towards the cold black waters beneath. I caught her by the waist. Pulled her back down. I broke a tendon in my knee when she landed on me but I held on until she stopped struggling. And I promised that if she lived, I'd be there. I'd give her my whole life, as long as she promised never to do that again. I'd put right all the problems in her life and be all that she could ever need. And we've never spoke about it since.

"I'm in it for the long haul," I say, evasively. "I promised."

I stop again. Realise how mad I sound. Stop myself and look at the clock. I probably shouldn't have left the lad. But he's confident. Self-assured. He grew up in a pub. He'll be fine.

She says nothing for a moment, then reaches down and pulls a notepad from her satchel. She writes something on the open page, but whether it is some clinical insight, or a reminder to pick up toilet rolls on the way home, I can't tell.

"What is it you want, David?"

"I want to matter. I want to be remarkable."

"To whom?"

"To everybody. To the people who doubt me."

"To the people who bullied you?"

"I doubt they even read."

"So why put all your energies and sense of self into becoming an author?"

"It's not for them. It's for me. It's so I know I'm not a fraud. That it wasn't just something nice to say to an unremarkable kid who knew how to write a decent poem."

"And you think you'll feel better if you get a book deal?"

"I can't feel any worse."

When her alarm sounds, it sounds a lot like God laughing.

20

Life, the Afterlife and Everything In Between

I think I believe in God.

No, scratch that, I definitely do believe in God. I've made my mind up and it's too draining to change my mind. Anyway, agnostics are just hedging their bets. I certainly believe in Something. And that Something could very well be God. Or Allah. Or Vishnu. Or Odin. Or the sunrise and stardust and the warm feeling you get when you remember your nan.

There are caveats, of course. I can't really get behind Old Testament God. I don't think that God wants us to hurt one another. I don't think They need us to be willing to sacrifice our children and endure all the torments of the Spanish Inquisition just to prove that we think They are really super awesome. I don't think that He (or She or They) is some Human-shaped attention junkie sitting on a cloud and throwing down cancers and Lottery wins based on who gives them the most adoration. Of course, I'll look a right dickhead come Judgement Day if the Amish have got it right, but I'm used to looking a dickhead and can't imagine that Satan will be able to do much to my disembodied soul, what with it having no nerve endings with which to feel pain. Then again, I can't get my head around how electricity works or why Australians don't fall off the planet or how we know that the wind isn't caused by all the trees thrashing about. So I'm probably not the most reliable person to ask.

I do know that I have always prayed, and that praying is something we should all make the time to do, whether it's through meditation or deep thought or just a gentle chat with the air and the trees and the dawn. It's important. It's useful. You don't need to thrash your back as you do it. It took me a while to get it right and to stop feeling compelled to get on my knees and clasp my hands and beg for forgiveness for every rude thought or disloyal impulse. I think it came as a relief to God. It sounded very maudlin, even to my ears, and I had no doubt that He/She/They would prefer to hear something less similar. That is, after all, why they've got such an interest in Original Sin. At least it's something new.

I prayed in my teens. I prayed to be left alone, and when that didn't work, I prayed for the strength to endure. Sometimes I prayed for my abusers to be struck down, though I'd always realise how horrid that was and rescind it before the morning. I'd pray for Dad to be happy and for Mam to worry less. I'd pray for my little brother to be just, well, generally safe and blessed. I'd pray that my grandparents would all live for years and years. I'd pray to get good marks in my exams. It became more about identifying what mattered to me. I prayed to be forgiven for things that I'd willingly done wrong. I'd pray to say thank-you for the good things in my life; for the beauty in the world and the ability to see it. I'd pray that He/She/They would look upon me softly and permit me to make mistakes without punishing me with the death of somebody important. I prayed for the visions to stop plaguing me, and then I prayed for understanding as to what they were. I never got a reply. Sometimes the voices in my head would tease me and pretend to be god, but I can always tell when the piss is being taken.

I do recall that I became firm in my belief in God when I was ten or eleven-years-old. Dad was putting the worst of the past few months behind him. I'd recently decided I wanted to be "really into" the world of golf. He'd promised that the next time he had the chance for a half day at work and I was off school, he'd take me down to the golf course in town. He'd have to walk home from work to get me and we'd have to walk the three miles there and back together, but we were no strangers to a hike and it sounded absolutely brilliant.

He picked a day midweek in the school holidays. We'd go on the Wednesday, he said. I was genuinely bouncing off the walls with excitement the night before. Mam kept saying there was rain forecast but Dad said that if it rained, we'd just get wet. And it did rain. Wednesday morning and the skies dark as a coal-miner's bathwater. It would be madness, said Mam. There's no way you can go golfing in this. There's no way.

I knew what was going to happen. She'd tell Dad it was too wet and he'd tell me we'd go another day, and then we wouldn't. And the thought of it was just too unbearable. The thought of not going was like a fistful of knives digging right inside my chest. So I prayed. I'd been in the cathedral choir for a few months and knew what was expected of me, and I literally clasped my hands together and begged and pleaded with the almighty to make my Dad ring home and tell her that we were going, and that was that. Please God, I begged. Before I count to ten, please let dad ring …

He did. The phone rang while I was counting. And he spoke with Mam for ages. Then she came in through the same door she'd burst in through to tell me he'd tried to kill himself, and said that we were both off our rockers, but he was coming home to get me and I'd need to wear clothes that could get ruined.

It was one of the best days I've ever had. The rain fell like an upright sea. We could barely see the golf balls and Dad managed to send a clod of turf flying 100 yards with a borrowed seven-iron. We got so wet it became funny. At one point, dad spat and told me that his saliva was drier than he was, and it was the funniest thing I'd ever heard. We sang songs by Wet, Wet, Wet. Even the lads who ran the club-shop shook their heads in amusement at the idea that we would be playing in weather so bad that half the plants in the garden disappeared into the soil and were never seen again. But we did, and it was wonderful. I was Ian Woosnam and he was Jack Nicklaus. I was good at putting. We picked up so many lost golf balls it looked like we were smuggling hard-boiled eggs in our pockets. It did, truly, make me believe in God. People have tried to take that belief away from me. I don't mind. Neither does God, I think. I view them very much as a slightly negligent aquarium-owner, occasionally remembering to change the filter and top up the feed and offering a rueful 'tssk' whenever one of the species pops its clogs. I do recall once praying with my headphones on and stopping talking so that God could enjoy some Metallica. If that's a sin, consider me sinful.

Heaven? Hell? Not a clue, which is a tricky thing to admit given my decades of suicidal ideation. What's awaiting? No idea.

I don't pray for 'things' any more. I just pray to say thank-you, and to ask for strength, and in the hope that I'm doing okay and that He/She/They doesn't look upon the species based on the worst of us. I find it quite peaceful. I like the silence. There's a quality to the silence when you're talking to God that suggests it matters, on some level – that somebody, somewhere, might actually be paying attention. I still thank Them for the golf.

21

Things That Aren't Real, and Things That Are

I'm driving too fast. I know I'm driving too fast but I like the feeling of rebellion, of social mutiny, so I keep my foot to the floor. I can't feel my foot, as it's made of keratin, of compacted hair, but the pedal isn't there either as the car is made of the coconut fibre that people use to slide down helter-skelters. I can't see very well but I can tell that the road beneath the tyres is slowly becoming a strange reptilian skin: red and black and magenta and each individual scale is edged with little thorns. The steering wheel is snakeskin too: a live snake, eating its own tail, but that doesn't matter as my hands are suddenly just tar-black stumps, stopping at the wrist in a nub of twisted plastic, the way pens go when you hold them to a lighter.

I can see the Humber Bridge up ahead. It's a dragon's back: the huge steel towers transformed into the peaks of its armoured spine. I'm driving on its neck. I'm handless, and I'm driving on a dragon's neck, and the water beneath the bridge isn't water any more, but a drawing of water, so I can see each individual pencil stroke, but the artist is clearly different to the one who drew the dragon, so I realise the dragon must be real and the river synthetic, which means somebody's messing me about. And now I'm inside my own mind and holding up porridgy blobs of my own grey matter in my somehow re-attached hands, and it all seems suddenly insane. None of this is real, I tell myself. This is all a fiction. A projection. A vision. I may as well lift my stumps from the wheel and let the car go in whichever direction it wants as there will be no consequences nothing else matters anyway…

And then Elora is telling me about something that's happening at school and asking if she can change the station on the radio, and I'm driving the Mitsubishi at a normal speed on a normal road and drifting towards the bridge in a line of unremarkable traffic and everything that I've just been witnessing has dwindled down to a little snow-globe that's sitting on the dashboard, and I can see myself, and my stump-hands, and the sports car driving up the dragon.

I started seeing things that weren't there when I was six or seven. I had an ear operation and needed my adenoids removed and I was given gas to knock me out for the operation. Apparently this can't possibly be true, but I remember spending days and weeks and months within the hideous multi-coloured swirl of colours and blobs and apparitions that bubbled up in the moments before I went unconscious. Apparently, it's normal to see weird stuff when you're going unconscious. But it wasn't weird. It was ugly and utterly terrifying. It was a horror movie and a science fiction film rolled into one. I was there for what seemed like an eternity, floating inside a starscape that roiled and burned and bubbled and folded inside itself and which chewed me and digested me and spat me out reborn an infinite amount of times. It was the worst thing I had ever experienced and to this day I believe I travelled somewhere and brought something bad back with me. I saw the same things when I experienced a high temperature: teeth and hair and faceless scribbled shapes. They came in my teenage years when I was terrified to go to school and the bullies used to kick lumps out of me. I'd see faceless wraiths: wisps of grey encased in monk cowls and they would watch, wordlessly, as I suffered my torments.

At 14, I saw death. The real one. Scythe, skull, burning eyes. I was laying on the sofa with my leg in plaster and I woke up to see him slicing down with his gleaming blade. I rolled out of the way and hurt my bad leg. As Mam came to pick me off the floor, he kept hacking down at me. I wrapped my arms around my head and she panicked that I was going mad and she told me she loved me and that it was all just because I was under a lot of stress and had a wonderful imagination and that I should write it all down. Maybe it would help me become a writer ...

I still see them. I hear them. I've joined little groups from time to time, sharing stories with like-minded people who have endured bouts of psychotic depression. They hear voices. See things that aren't there. We see different things. We hear different things. I once met a chap who could hear the actor Derek Jacobi reciting lines in the very centre of his head. Mine are simpler, with the exception of the Roman centurion who keeps reading out names in some abomination of street-Latin. I hear my name a lot. I hear laughter. Sometimes there are little whispered suggestions. I don't get as much abuse as I used to but I see vastly more abominations in those brief spells when I'm not writing a new book. Those are the times when I have dreams, too. When I'm writing, I don't dream at all.

This is the hardest bit to write about. I know it sounds like I'm genuinely out of my mind. I've no doubt you're thinking that it must have been a really bad idea to experiment with drink and drugs when I was already so given to hallucination. And yes, you're probably right. There's something about intoxicants that break down barriers and inhibitions. They cause a proper riot in the maximum security prison in my head, in such moments, the lunatics are out of their cages and running wild and I can do nothing but hold on and ride it out and hope I don't do anything bad in a spirit of joining in.

There's not a lot you can say to somebody in the midst of a psychotic episode. Really, all I can encourage you to do is to keep yourself safe and try to give them a comfortable space where they can put themselves back together. But the everyday stuff? The weird goblins and the swarms of bats and the sense that the road is turning into ink beneath your feet? Most people find a space for it all within themselves. I can differentiate between the real and the imagined. I can ignore the little monsters shouting for my attention. I can dismiss the most paranoid of my imaginings and feel reasonably sure that this is real, and I'm writing it with my own fingers, and that I'm not one of the voices in a head belonging to somebody else.

If nothing else, it helps me be a better writer. And that's what I stayed alive to become. Perhaps Hell is empty and all the devils are in me. Perhaps I'm mad and simply haven't done anything irredeemable yet. Or maybe none of this happened and I'm making it up for sympathy. All feel equally true.

22

Go On, Have a Rummage

Social media posting, *June 2021.*

So ...

I'm severely bi-polar. I suffer bouts of depression that turn me into a vinegary porridge of utter, irreversible wretchedness. I'm an alcoholic in recovery. I've suffered bouts of debilitating Obsessive Compulsive Disorder, I experience auditory and visual hallucinations and live with the whisper of suicidal ideation at the periphery of my thoughts. I've got so much more wrong than right.

Despite that, I'm a cheerful, feisty sod and I genuinely try not to let my brain get me down. I keep going, and believe in myself. I have many, many questions about the world, my place within it, and I have very few answers. Where, for example, does my personality end and my illness begin? When does being sad become being ill? How much suffering does a person have to endure before they 'qualify' for society's compassion?

As such, I'm busily putting the finishing touches to a very personal memoir about three decades of living with my various mental passengers. It's going to be offering a look into all the shadows and recesses of a head that, apparently, isn't very well. I want to make sure it's useful. So now would be the time to ask any questions you may have about living with any one of the many things that are wrong with me. Don't be in the slightest bit afraid to ask. I don't get offended and am pathologically honest about things like this, if a little glib about the rest of my reality. So if you think there's something it should contain, do shout up. It's as much for the people who don't have depression as for those that do.

- **As a recovered alcoholic, what's your advice to those dealing with an addict?**
  Patience is key. It's important to remember that the addiction is more powerful than any other force. It's insidious, but it floods you to the point that every decision you make is designed to convince yourself it's okay to indulge. For me, it was about finding something more important to me than drink, and that took years and years and

lots of false starts. Showing somebody their worth is a good place to start. Try and steer clear of making somebody feel shame, as it literally reinforces all the bad feeling. And applaud the little steps. Show them that they're moving on the right path. It's the hardest battle anybody can fight and believing that somebody really is there to help you can be a real breakthrough. And finally, know your boundaries. Decide how much you can endure. You owe it to yourself to give as much of yourself as you can, but some addicts really will take more than you can safely give.

- **How long have you been sober?**

14 months. I gave up drinking on New Year's Day 2017 and went an entire year without a sip of alcohol, having been a bottle-of-whisky-a-day man for a decade previous. But slowly it began to creep back into my life. I'd told myself as long as I stayed clear of whisky I would be sticking to my vow not to 'drink' again, but it just meant I started drinking stronger and stronger cider, then moving onto brandy and rum, and soon drinking was in my thoughts and in my life all the time again. I functioned, but it turns out I was never really fooling anybody. My addiction kept telling me it was okay, it was making me a better person, a more loving partner, a more giving dad. One night I was writing and drinking rum from the bottle and I caught sight of myself in the reflection of the computer and was so overcome with self-loathing that I literally wanted to die. And the only thing that said it understood, was the bottle. I left a self-pitying post on Facebook and just collapsed in on myself in a drunken, sobbing mess for my partner to find. The next day I saw how many positive messages I'd been sent and how worried my littlest girl had been when she saw me, and that was it. No more drinking of any kind. I will always want to but for the first time ever, I really do now know that I won't.

- **If you mention Obsessive Compulsive Disorder at all could you make it clear it's more than liking things clean or in order. It can manifest in many strange ways.**

It's utterly debilitating. The cleanliness and order were irrelevant to me. Mine was all about rituals and private superstitions that overtook my every thought. I'd find myself writing transcripts of conversation on my leg using a finger-pencil. I had to obsessively clear my throat;

turn the taps in a set order while brushing my teeth; say a specific set of words in a set order while saying goodbye to a loved one through fear that they would die if I didn't. I'd have a panic attack if I didn't see a specific amount of postal vans on my drive to work. I got better when I started taking a firmer hold of sanity. That sounds very glib but I had to make a conscious decision simply not to do the things that gifted me these false shields against fear. It was a harder battle than giving up drink.

- **How to talk to children about someone who has mental health issues. I know it depends on their ages, but... any thoughts?**

No differently to the way you would talk about any other illness. You have to take it easy with your cousin because they have really bad asthma. Don't jump on Auntie Julie as she has osteoporosis. And if you see so-and-so, just remind them how much they mean to you as they're really struggling right now. Kids are a lot less judgemental than adults. I asked my three year old what he would say to somebody who was feeling horribly sad. She said she would give them a hug and tell them they had shine. I rather liked that.

- **How do you deal with unreasonable anger especially if you think it might get you in trouble, and how can you make others see that it's part of the mental health condition and not who you are?**

The anger is a symptom of something deeper. Nobody is born with rage inside them. It really is about learning to recognise the mounting symptoms and identifying the triggers before you explode. Be clear with those who love you that you're going through some stuff and may fly off the handle, but do try and remember that your behaviour does inevitably impact on those around you, even if it does come from a dark place inside. I've got much better at removing myself from situations that might be triggering but it all comes down to turning your frustration into a fuel that will assist you rather than a fire that burns through your life.

- **Have you come across people who simply refuse to acknowledge that you have an illness? I have a friend whose partner "does not believe in depression" and insists that he is fine even though he is patently not at all fine some days.**

Human beings aren't great at changing their minds. Denial comes very easily to some people. Accepting that something is wrong can be a daunting thing to consider so it's far better to some people that they keep their guard up and their self-destructive coping mechanisms in place, and keep their pain bottled up. For lots of people, it's a sign of strength. Slowly, society is changing its perceptions. It's now seen as more courageous to ask for help. That is a huge step. All I can really suggest is that your friend keep finding ways to tell her partner that they don't judge them or think less of them and that they will be there for them throughout what is sure to be a difficult time. We have to stop expecting so much of ourselves and each other. We're all a bit broken in one way or another and fixing ourselves shouldn't be seen as an irritant to those around us. Sometimes it does feel as though people have got a limited amount of compassion. They may be very considerate at first but when they ask 'how are you feeling' it can feel as though they're asking 'are you not better yet?''. It's a long, slow, painful process. Your friend might do well to tell their partner that they know they have the strength to take that frightening journey.

- **Mental health provision, or lack thereof. As someone who has experience of "the system" first hand and as a parent, I'm interested to know how difficult or easy it was for you to obtain diagnoses and support over the years from the health service. And also whether that's changed for the better or worse.**

Getting help is a gruelling undertaking these days, and invariably undertaken at a time when you are feeling your weakest and least up to the task. It used to be that a trip to the GP would lead to an assessment with a mental health professional and then quickly in to the right type of therapy. There even used to be respite beds available for people afraid they might hurt themselves. None of that now. The waiting time for accessing therapy is endless and they guard the phone number of the crisis teams as if its treasure. I have no swifter access to help than somebody who has never suffered with mental health difficulties before. I've been told by an A and E nurse that my best bet is to go to a suicide spot and let myself be talked down and that will move me up the list. Not joking. I've paid for private counselling in the past to be able to get help quicker, which offends my socialism.

But when you miss a payment it becomes a whole different relationship and very much about the money. So, in essence, it's bloody awful.

- **I have never been able to comprehend why anyone would consider suicide. However, I live with someone who has more than thought about it. Someone who thinks about it on a daily basis. My question is, what's the best way to help someone in that position?**

Once suicide creeps into your thoughts it is so hard to get it to leave. It's almost an addiction in the way it overtakes all else. All you can do as a friend is to listen, to be there, and to show how much you believe in their ability to get well. Show that you're listening, don't get impatient and let them see that whatever they need, you are there to help give them strength. It's draining and hard, but never forget that it's always so much harder for those experiencing it, however hard it might be for those around them.

23.

In Sanity

The doctor is far too pretty to be honest with. I know that as soon as she calls my name and I stumble, bleary-eyed, into the cosy little room at the end of the long, too-bright corridor. I know how I'm going to act for the next five minutes: witty, irreverent, utterly false. I wish to God I could view her dispassionately: a professional, a grown-up, a highly-proficient GP. But all I can see is somebody who's infinitely better than me, and who I know I am about to try and impress. She's round about my age and looks as though she's really got her act together. Her parents must be so proud. I know at once that she's travelled. She's probably got a gorgeous house. I imagine she writes poetry and plays the harp. I bet she watches old movies and cries just the right amount of tears at the sad parts. I feel like the dog-turd on the soul of her expensive shoe and all she's done is call my name and smile at me and tell me she's sorry about making me wait. I can't tell her the truth. I'm already so far beneath her that it makes me numb and angry all at once. I know that her training won't allow her to think ill of me, but the truth of her, the essence of who she is, will impulsively see me as weak, self-pitying and hopelessly mad. This is going to be excruciating. I have to say something funny. Something clever. Something coarse, if it helps to distract her from the mess that's slumped in her swivel chair.

I was supposed to see the other doctor – the laid back, grey-haired chap who once told me that everybody gets down sometimes and that I should probably spend more time in nature and think about drinking less. I don't really care what he thinks of me so I have no compunction about being honest. I have every intention of telling him that I can't eat and can't sleep and feel panicky and miserable all at once and that for the past few weeks I've been seeing all sorts of horrific hallucinations: that the pills he put me on six months ago don't seem to be working.

Instead I've got the locum. Early thirties. Long brown hair and incredible blue eyes. Short tweed skirt, heeled brogues, white blouse and a fun little cardigan. Her bag, propped beneath the desk, has a diamante-studded skull on the side. She's cool and clever and her smile seems genuine as I bumble through the door and plonk myself down on the little chair.

I've got myself in the right state of mind to come out with it. I see things that aren't there, Doc. I can hear voices again. I keep seeing Death. Every shadow has a cowl and I feel as though a greasy rusted scythe is about to slash down and cut me adrift. I want to die, but not like this, not now, not with Elora getting bigger and better and liking me the way she does …

I tell her I'm feeling a bit down in the dumps still. The pills might be helping or they might not, it's hard to say. I start talking, in that way of mine, which makes people look as if they're a bit nervous and overwhelmed.

I can't say if I'm depressed. I mean, life's so hard, isn't it? I'm struggling on the money front. My partner and me argue all the time, but I think that's to do with the money and there's no cash available on prescription, is there? I feel regret a lot but then I tell myself I'm not the sort of person who looks back, and I try looking forward again, but there doesn't seem to be anything on the horizon to get excited about. I've heard nothing about my books for months. I've always got indigestion and headaches and yeah, I'm drinking lots, but life's just better after a drink or two, isn't it? What's the alternative? And yeah, I sleep now and again, though I don't really like it. My partner says I hold myself really tight in weird positions when I'm sleeping and I wake up with aches all down my shoulders and in my jaw. But I'm doing what I need to. I see my daughter every day. She's with me half the time now and she's just all the light and love and gold in my life. I want to make her proud, so that has to be good. I don't let myself think about stuff that will make me gloomy. I keep busy, so that's all good, isn't it? Being industrious, tiring yourself out …

She stops me before I run out of things to say. Works through it a little bit at a time. at one point she picks up the phone and asks the receptionist to re-book our session as a double appointment. She gives me time. And I talk some more.

It's the seeing things that frightens me. It's all the time. I can always tell what's real and what's not, but sometimes I'll be driving and I'll genuinely see great flocks of birds smashing into my windscreen in a great mess of snow and hail and feathers and blood, and I have to not look at it, but then it means I'm doing 60mph with my eyes closed. But if I stop driving I can't get work and if I can't get work I can't support my family and if I can't do that then what use am i? And if I'm no use, I might as well not be here. But I made a promise that I would stay alive. So I just need to be able to control the voices and the visions so they only bother me when it doesn't affect anybody else. I can take that. I'll take whatever the universe wants me to endure. But I don't want to hurt the people I care about, and I'm frightened ...

She changes the dosage of my pills. Adds an anti-psychotic to my repeat prescription. Tells me she's made an immediate referral to the psychiatric team for assessment and more talking therapies, though she warns me there will be a long wait. She urges me to drink less and sleep more – the visions being more vibrant when I'm exhausted. She tells me it will pass. There's a certainty in the way she says it. She reassures me that there's nothing on my medical records that suggests I'm a danger to anybody. I'm bi-polar, obviously. This is the first time I've heard it put this way. I thought I was a manic depressive this morning. "Bi-polar," I muse. "Sounds like I fancy two big white bears".

The next time I see her it's to do with a painful in-growing hair at the bottom of my back. We don't discuss my mental health. I insist she write in my notes that it's a *'growth on my hip'*. I notice her write *'boil on buttock'* and make her change it. I still have some pride, after all.

She asks me how I'm feeling in myself. If I'm still writing. Tells me that it might do me some good to put my thoughts and feelings down on paper. She gives herself a pat on the back for astuteness when I tell her that I've got a literary agent and we're waiting to hear back regarding a manuscript that's been sent out to a few commissioning editors.

"There you go, then," she says. "So much to look forward to. Be positive – the universe might hear you".

I drive home in tears. That's why I haven't heard any good news, of course. I've been too obsessed with myself. Festering inside my own misery. I need to get better at looking positive; at brimming with enthusiasm. I have to stop short of looking manic, lest somebody see through the façade. I go home, open a bottle of whisky and set about looking confident, capable and ready for whatever occurs. I can do positivity. I can keep my effervescence sizzling. I can tell all and sundry that I'm about to become the next big thing in publishing. I'm gifted, after all. I'm one of the true greats. I'm dreadful at lots of things but I compensate by being truly blessed at three specific things. I'm a brilliant writer, a spectacular lover, and I'm really good at making omelettes. It's a line that always gets a laugh. I'm still using it on stage a decade later, promoting the latest of my critically-acclaimed, commercially-disastrous novels. My sales figures are 'toxic' according to my last agent. I'd be more attractive to commissioning editors if I was a debut novelist. Ten years as a published novelist and I'm further behind the starting line than I was when I began.

But I'm okay about it. I don't feel the urge to show boundless reserves of positivity. I just write the books, and enjoy the process, and say thank-you when readers and reviewers tell me I'm marvellous. It's enough. It might not be tomorrow, but it is today.

24.

Wham, Bam, Thanks Mam

I'm pushing 30. A bit too fat. An alcoholic, though I haven't realized it yet. I'm smoking again. Self-employed, though it feels more like 'jobless'. I've walked out of my reporting job after an argument with the new editor and am doing little bits of freelance work here and there. It brings in about a tenth of what we need. Elora is staying with me half the time and with her mum the other half. She's brilliant. Sometimes I just sit and look at her and feel my heart slow down. I talk to her about how sad I get and she gives me 'big cuddles' and tells me she loves me six times an hour, as requested. We play adventure games. She comes to the pub with me. She gets on with my new partner but has a tendency to act up if I'm not giving her my complete attention. She gets a couple of smacks on the bottom from my girlfriend when she refuses to sit on the naughty step, and I don't intervene because my girlfriend is older, and has a nice kid, so must know what she's doing. Elora rips up her voile curtains and pees her bed in protest. A battle of wills will continue for the next nine years. It's okay, in a way. We're not living in the pub any more. I've bought a house, though I'll lose it pretty soon. My stepson has won a scholarship to boarding school but it's still expensive, and I've gone through the profits of the house sale trying to find a lifestyle that I've promised, but which I can't afford. We don't see as much of him. It's just me and his mum, and our house, and the bills. I'm writing a book that I think might do okay. It feels very real to me; very authentic, and I'm letting cigarettes burn down to the filter in the ashtray as I pound out page after page of death and blood and bile. I'm paying for my own therapy. Fifty quid a week, which I can't afford. I've spent all the money from the sale of the house. Bankruptcy's looming. In a few weeks my brother will fall out with me because I'll borrow some money and not pay it back. He'll be within his rights, of course, but I'll take it badly. Doesn't he realise what I'm going through? Doesn't he see how hard I'm trying? I'll sell my saxophone, just to claim the moral high ground and pay it back and we won't talk until the day that dad brings us together in the pub and tells us he's got the cancer.

But now, here, today, I'm sitting in the back of my brother's car. Mam's in the front seat. She's 5ft and weighs 7 stone but she gets the senior position. I'm in the back with my brother's girlfriend. If anybody were to lick the condensation on the inside of the windows it would taste of this morning's whisky and last night's wrath. I'm trying my best to be whatever it is that normal people want me to be. So we're building Mam up. Telling her she's done really well to get herself out and about. She looks well. She's got some colour back in her cheeks. She's come down on the train on her own, which isn't really a big deal for me, what with having been a journalist since 17 and capable of tying my own shoelaces for quite a while. But she's anxious, is Mam. She gets nervous. Panicky. Jittery. Gets herself all het up. She likes things to be nice. To be just-so. She can see the potential pitfalls of every action and inaction. So getting herself here, to stay with my brother, is a win, after everything that's happened between her and Dad. My brother picked her up in Leeds, as it was asking a bit much for her to actually change trains in her condition, but she's here. Praise the Lord.

It's hard work for me. I haven't got a persona that works in her company. My jokes are too crude or too silly. I sound insincere in my compliments. The things I'm excited about sound like pipe dreams. I've got my priorities all wrong. She loves me, but I drive her up the bloody wall. I haven't got a single anecdote about my current life that doesn't lead to some kind of passive aggressive diatribe on my morality. She couldn't live like me. She doesn't know anybody who could live like me. She doesn't mean it as a compliment, so I pretend to take it like one. The voices in my head go quiet when she's here. The one that talks in her voice occasionally nods in the recesses of my skull, but the rest just slink back into the shadows. They've all been quieter, of late. The whisky shuts them up. They seem to like me more now I'm behaving like the bastard they always knew me to be. I go by "Marko" now. David is dead and buried.

She's telling us her plans for the next day. My brother's got something on in the morning, and I say I have to, and she's telling him not to worry, she'll just stay in his flat and keep herself busy with something or other, and that it's not a worry, and she has her book.

"You'd enjoy the art gallery," I tell her. "There's some great exhibitions on."

She tells us she'll be fine, she'd never find it. I tell her it's literally ten minutes away and of course she'll find it. The people who run it know me, actually, and if she mentions my name she might even get a guided tour. She rolls her eyes, as if I'm either completely deluded or showing off. I prickle. Tell her more stuff about the esteem which I'm fortunate enough to enjoy thanks entirely to having been a local journalist for years. I get free tickets, and I don't have to queue and people whisk me to the front of the line, and I even got a complimentary lap-dance when they opened The Purple Door, and the mood takes a dark turn. My brother's laughing, nervously, because he can see how hard this is going to be. She approves of my brother. He's nice. Stayed in school. Went to university. Sensitive, but really caring.

"The restaurant is really nice too. You could have some breakfast in there then see the exhibition…,"

She tells me she'll be happy doing what she's already planned.

Then we have the little exchange that will live in my head, playing on a loop, for years.

"But you could be happier, Mam…,"

"That's your problem, David – you always want to be happier."

At the time it's so patently absurd that I literally cannot stop myself from laughing out loud. Yeah, that's a major problem, isn't it? Wanting to be happier? What an extraordinarily twattish dream. How selfish and self-aggrandizing to want to feel more joy. It's a sentence I repeat, over and over, in the pub that afternoon, finding ways to drop it into conversation with regulars and strangers and willing them to be as visibly appalled by the sentiment as I am. I want her to be laughable. Because if she is, all the other stuff she thinks about me and my personality will be invalidated by association. The diplomats tell me she was probably just too nervous to go out on her own, but I don't want to hear it. I'm sneeringly angry at her for being so bloody feeble and yet having such a hold on how I think about myself. She's too scared to do anything and I do every single thing that scares me and yet she still has the temerity to judge me? No wonder Dad left. No wonder her sons live 150 miles away.

I think of it differently now, of course. I look back at the 'me' of that time and I hate him in the way that I should have hated myself at the time. I never lacked self-loathing but in those days it was pointing in the wrong direction. I was despising my weakness, my vulnerabilities, my inability to persuade the world of my absolute superiority. I held my toughness, my fortitude, my willingness to do what it took; my badness – they were the aspects of myself that felt most real and aspirational and they were the characteristics I made damn sure I exhibited. It didn't take more than a glancing connection for her to send waves of feeling through my every nerve ending. Her disapproval cut as deeply as it did when I was a kid and had been hanging out with the bad lads, or I'd been seen kissing my girlfriend by the phonebox and making a show of myself. It was the eye roll that did it – the presumption that I was trying to make myself sound good and influential when we both knew I was a loser who'd thrown away everything I had in pursuit of something a little like happiness.

A few years later I was driving her through to Leeds to get the bus back to Carlisle, and she asked me how my mental health was faring. I reminded her of what she'd said and she told me what she'd probably meant. She hadn't given it any further thought and she was sorry if it had upset me. She told me she loved me and was proud of me but it's not easy seeing your son making decisions you don't agree with.

I didn't plan to cry. I was trying to navigate the Leeds ring-road and she's never trusted my driving so she was gripping the fabric of the passenger seat as if she were dangling from a tightrope. And I just came out and told her that yeah, I know she loves me, but it's duty, it's DNA, it's written into her code that she must love her own offspring, but that I'd like her to love 'me', the individual, the personality, the person. And she said that she did. The bloody floodgates opened. I said something I didn't even know I felt. I said I wanted to be somebody's priority. I wanted to be loved 'best'., To be loved 'most'. And she cried and said she didn't know what I meant, and I could barely see for all the snot and tears, and then I sorted myself out because she was due on the bus and I didn't want her going back to Carlisle feeling all upset.

I still don't really know what I meant. But I'm pleased I pursued 'happier'. I'm pleased she did too. I've never really told her how bad the depression gets or how desperately I've wanted permission to simply stop existing. I think she probably knows. She likes 'me' much better now. I'm more like her David, whatever that might mean. Sobriety probably helps. And I'm much less of a twat. I just wish she'd been able to acknowledge just how good I was at being that twat. It was the performance of a lifetime, and I got zero credit.

When I talk about all this in therapy, the psychologists usually stop taking notes. Some things are just too tangled to be unknotted.

25.

A Bridge Too Far

January, 2005.

A Wednesday night.

11.58pm.

The car park by the bridge.

David Mark. Senior reporter for the Yorkshire Post. Married man. A father, now. Grade 6 saxophone and Grade 5 clarinet. 100 words per minute in Teeline shorthand. Homeowner. Dreamer. Loser.

Look at him. Glasses. Receding hair. Paunch. Space-hopper face. Bunched up like an arthritic fist in the driver's seat of the new Vauxhall Zafira. It's a people-carrier, to make room for the baby and all her stuff. A status-symbol, to some. Practical, according to the salesman.

He's not crying. He wants to. Would love to. There's a peach-stone in his throat and cold grit in his eyes, but the tears won't fall so he just pulls anguished faces and rubs his face with his gloved hands. Wonders how hard he would have to hit himself in the chest to stop his own heart. Whether life can be ceased by will alone.

The dark crescent beneath his right eye sings with pain as he jabs his thumb into it.

He does it again.

And again.

His wife's face swimming in his vision. His own, too, inches from hers.

He shivers again. He doesn't want to put the blowers on. Normally he would sit and curse the weather but tonight the cold is almost comforting, the goose pimples on his skin a physical reminder of the unpleasantness of it all.

Not long now.

Minutes, maybe. Then the kiss and splash. The proof that he wasn't just looking for attention. That he meant it when he said she was better off without him. That they all are.

Moments more.

Then blessed nothingness.

He looks at his watch. Seconds from midnight.

He steps out onto the tarmac, the sudden gust of icy wind filling the car and blowing his scarf up over his face. The wind is stirring the carpet of leaves and bending the trees that surround the empty car park. The gusts almost mask the sounds of the cars swishing by on the bridge overhead.

It's a nasty night and he pulls a face, huddling into his black coat. It's a wool and cashmere blend with a burgundy lining, but he tells people it's all cashmere.

The gnawing hunger in his gut kicks against his insides and he belches, filling his mouth with the taste of his own bile and bitterness. He's barely eaten in weeks, and sickness has become a constant. He vomits at thoughts he don't like; at new situations and pressing engagements. It's a nervous condition, so the doctors say. He's disassociated himself from his own body. His gut belongs to his head, and his head doesn't belong to him.

He wipes his mouth, and spits. The inside of his face is sore, tense.

His nasal passages tingling.

Ribs aching.

Migraine, like a band around his face, forcing his to hold his head still: his neck aching as a consequence.

A few street lamps are still on, casting a sickly sodium glow over a landscape of empty parking spaces.

The Humber Bridge Country Park.

He's parked close to the woods, near the admin offices. 12 hours ago the place would have been buzzing, despite the weather. It's a haven of sorts. Deep lakes, green with algae and punctured by fallen branches that poke through its surface like so many blades. 50-foot limestone cliffs, dirtied by moss. Well-groomed forests of ash and sycamore, parted like Brylcremed hair with man-made paths and helpful hand-rails. Nature, tamed.

They used to walk miles in its cosy embrace. Laughing. Loving. Reciting baby names. Listing holiday destinations and favourite meals. Wrapped up in the bollocks of it all. Talking and planning and pretending and unburdening. Her, listening and nodding and pretending and not comprehending, and wishing he was normal and loving that he wasn't; ever walking on the rice paper and egg-shells of his temper.

They always take the same route through the acres of gentle forest, before winding their way up the slopes, through the car park and then back across the road to the footpath and cycle track which slope up to the bridge; 500,000 tonnes of steel and concrete, stitching East Yorkshire to North Lincolnshire.

She would always be too tired to walk right across the bridge into Barton, so she would head back to the car while he jogged half-way across its girth and looked down on the turgid brown waters of the Humber below. Losing himself in fantasy for a while. Wondering how it would feel to climb over the railing and let gravity do its worst.

His watch beeps suddenly as night turns into morning.

It is the day of his death.

He locks the car out of habit and drop the keys into the depths of his pocket, where they find a comfortable spot between his note-book, cigarettes and mobile phone.

He looks up at the bridge, and gives a smile. Once upon a time he would have checked himself in the car window for aesthetic perfection, but he can't stand his reflection. He stopped looking at himself weeks ago.

He looks up at the bridge. Down at his shoes. Turns his head to the right where the footpath that he and his wife used to take is shrouded in darkness. The woods have no shape. Just a black mass; all whistling sounds and shaking branches, snapping twigs and falling leaves. They hold no danger for the damned. A man in pursuit of his own death doesn't fear ambush.

Some part of himself remarks on the solitude; the absence of anybody else with death on their mind. There should be a fucking queue.

He looks again into the dark mouth of the forest, and snarls, as if its an opponent to be intimidated. Shows his teeth. Spits.

Robotic, mechanical, almost unwilling, he turns and tramps off into the woods.

Curses himself for changing his plans. Asks what he's doing and hears the voices in his head shriek with anger. They didn't want to push him this far.

He doesn't want to prolong his life for even a moment longer. He doesn't want to feel this way, or any way, any more. He wears misery the way beautiful people wear clothes. His brain recoils from every new vista and experience like a salted slug. He yearns for death. Longs for oblivion. But inside him, a voice is telling his he needs to feel his heart beat before he can stop it. To walk in the woods and tell the shadows to do their worst..

He has played out this journey in his head a thousand times: entertained the notion of death as one would think of a delicious dessert after an unpleasant main course. He knows the taste of every last breath of this fantasy. he knows every step. The slow, plodding walk up the pathway and the stairs to the bridge platform. He will be smoking a cigarette and breathing heavily; eyes wet, but not crying. Relaxed, he will walk past the guard on the toll booth, nod a curt greeting as he pretends he is walking home to Barton after a night out. He will gaze up at the lights which stud the girders and harp strings of the bridge, and perhaps allow himself to imagine, to lie, that they are steps to Heaven. He will reach the halfway point, finish his cigarette, · and pause for a moment, inhaling the world. The cold wind will be as razor blades on his face. his heart will be beating like two rams butting heads inside his chest. A car will drive by, with a pretty girl at the wheel, and he'll give her a shrug and a smile, for he is a man whom women find attractive. He will light another cigarette, breathe deep, to his toes. He will pull up the collar of his coat, remove his mobile phone from his pocket and place it on the wet walkway. Then he will close his eyes, place his hands on the cold metal rail, steels his nerve, give a grimace back over his shoulder at the world he is escaping and then leap, in one fluid movement, into the dark.

Thinking:

I will.

I will.

There will be a moment's exhilaration, an urge to exclaim, perhaps to scream....

He's in the moment, now. Excited by it. The wind tears at him, tugs at his coat, blows hot ash from his cigarette into his face, but cannot pull his back. He smiles as he hits the waters, elegant and brutal in the instant of collision.

The waters splinter as ice as they embrace him; his breath taken by the sudden grip of cold and dark, the mud and leaves in his mouth; then soothing, peaceful calm as he paddles away from the agony of it all, and is sucked into the treacle and tar of eternal sleep.

..and I die...

He wonders if in his final moments, the monsters will appear, and he can watch the beautiful bastards drown.

Already the woods have swallowed him up.

He can hear his own boots rustling through the wet leaves and keeps a hand on the rail as the footpath starts to descend. The forest is black and cold, and he can sense eyes upon him; hear the scrabbling claws of the creatures who live in the dark.

He feels as though he is walking inside himself .

His footsteps are becoming heavy, his coat starting to stoop his shoulders. Despite himself, he's starting to feel nervous. Beneath his gloves, the tips of his fingers are growing cold, and he starts making fists. His eyes are watering, forcing him to close them for longer and longer moments, inviting slumber, wrapping sleep around himself as a blanket against the cold.

The wind growing more distant as the branches above his head form a tangled, twisted screen.

He is lost now. Lost in the darkness. He reaches out his hand and feels the knobbled bark of a tree trunk. He realises his feet are wet, that water has soaked past the lip of his boots. He splashes backwards, onto soft ground. His right boot slips and his knee hits the wet ground, hard. His teeth bang together and he mashes the side of his tongue. He can taste blood. He spits on the forest floor, raising a gloved finger to his mouth. Even through the leather he can feel the wetness.

Now the tears flow. His throat coughs up a lump and he spits it on the forest floor as salt-water runs down his cheeks.

He doesn't sob. He doesn't give in to it, even now. Instead, he holds himself still: fists balled, teeth locked, as the tears pour down his face.

He's crying for what he is, for what lives within him. For the hurt he has caused. For all he has failed to do.

His cheeks feel raw as the wind slices against the tears and he wipes his face dry with the back of a glove. He screws up his eyes, peering again into the gloom. There are vague shapes, but nothing more. He takes a tentative step and realises his boots are now on soft leaves, rather than the hardness of the path. He shuffles forward again and strike something firm. He curses and stops again. His grand gesture, his heroic death, is becoming farce.

He sits in the dark for an hour. Thinks of the different ways this last journey could play out. Imagines how it would feel if he were to bump into some other wretchedly suicidal young man bumbling around in the dark. Would he let them go first, he wonders. Would he try and talk him out of it? Would they exchange war stories: mental scars? The beginnings of a narrative begins to form in his mind. A man such as he could easily blunder into some nefarious exchange, here, in the dark and the cold. Would he fight for his life were somebody to threaten it? Would saving a life persuade him to cherish his own?

He goes back to the car. The note is on the passenger seat where he left it. He lets the story build and build and realises it's a tale worth telling.

By the time he picks up his wife from her late shift, the plot is fully formed. He feels enthused. Excited. Manic, even. He tells her he's had an idea about a journalist who wants to kill himself and ends up involved in a murder plot.

"That'll be some light relief for you," she says, putting her seatbelt on.

***

Six months later, he's written it. And he's living with somebody else.

He's still alive, in his way.

But the man he was is still floating, blue-faced and bloated, in the deep dark waters of the Humber.

26

The Art of Staying Miserable When You've Got Everything You've Ever Wanted

I'm in the kitchen on the first floor: an office block that squats like a broken-down spaceship in the centre of this quiet east Yorkshire town.

I've been working for this news and features agency for six years. I hate it. Nobody really likes their job but I hate it so much that I've spent the past couple of years seeing just how far a person has to go to get sacked. It's the most pointless job I've ever had, writing TV highlights and the occasional profile on soap stars I've never heard of. It's about as far from real journalism as it's possible to get and still be able to put it on your business card. It's ten hour shifts, four days a week, and the people in charge expect you to actually be there, at your desk. I can't spread my workload out over the day like most of the other battery-chickens who peck away at their keyboards in this deathly quiet aircraft hangar. I'm usually finished by about half nine, so the rest of the day is spent trying to think of things to do until I'm allowed to go home. We get a half hour lunch, but I manage to stretch that out to long enough for three double whiskies and two pints of lager, which at least makes the afternoon shift slightly more tolerable. I spend huge amounts of the day watching children fall off trampolines on YouTube, or flirting via email with any one of a number of similarly jaded workmates. I quite like the members of my own little department, of which I am nominally second-in-command. I've started smoking again just to be allowed cigarette breaks. I'll run errands to the bakery for the entire department if it means getting away from my desk for long enough to breathe in some fresh air. I go to the town Minster every day, sitting in the cool air and breathing in that scent of wood polish and dust. I pray for change. I pray for anything that will change my life. I vow to take whatever punishment or sacrifice is required of me if I am just permitted some different kind of life. I see how long I can drive with my eyes closed on the way home. I pretend I've forgotten how many painkillers and anti-depressants I've already taken, just so I can knock back a few more with a half bottle of Bell's. It's not suicide if it's an accident, right?

So I'm in the kitchen, wedged up beside the vending machine, looking out at the traffic bastard who patrols the market place and gives out fines to anybody with a tyre half an inch over the line.

I'm on the phone to my agent. It's a strange feeling. I've had an agent for the past three years but we've parted ways without ever getting anywhere. Now I have another one. He gets me. Likes me, even. Seems to find my personality an asset. Decides we can probably play up the 'Northerner' thing. And he's ringing to tell me that there are now four publishing houses bidding for the UK rights to the book that is now called Dark Winter, and which was born during an aborted suicide attempt.

"They'll all be trying to persuade you to go with them" he says. "So just listen and ask any questions you want."

And this is it, really. This is the moment. Commissioning editors ringing me at work to tell me that they think my manuscript is 'masterful' and one of the most promising new crime thrillers that they've ever seen. And they're begging me to choose them. They know it will come down to the size of the offer, but they can all guarantee me that they're going to make me a household name.

My head's spinning with it all. Part of me is genuinely, definitively happy. This is, after all, what it's all been about. The 'Mam' in me is urging caution. If something's too good to be true then it probably is. Wait until it's all signed, sealed and delivered. Remember, Dave – you're not great with money…

I'm in and out of the kitchen all day. My boss is also my best friend and she's unbelievably pleased this is all happening for me, if only so she can stop having to deal with the complaints about me before they reach HR.

It doesn't actually come down to money in the end. Of the different offers on the table, I pick the second highest. Let's call it roughly £80,000 for two books. I'm familiar with the publishing house because they're making a fortune off the back of Girl with the Dragon Tattoo, which I've just read, and didn't mind. They explain how the payments work, and I don't really listen. Payment upon signature, payment upon delivery of the manuscript, payment upon hardback release and payment upon paperback release – the process to be replicated with book two. My agent will take 15 per cent. Apparently I'll be taxed on whatever I do get and under no circumstances should I think about quitting work until I'm properly established. It could be 18 months before the book comes out and anything could happen.

I phone my partner. She screams, in a good way. She tells the kids before I get to them and they've got hugs for me aplenty when we meet up for a celebratory sausage-in-a-basket at the little country pub where we sometimes go.

We go up to Carlisle for the weekend so I can tell my parents at the same time. There's much squealing. My brother gives me a huge hug. My grandparents say they knew I could do it – my nana even revealing some old yellow newspaper clippings from my first newspaper column on the local paper. Elora's mum is so pleased for me she seems like she could burst.

I only really get some peace and quiet to digest it all when I'm saying my prayers. I don't know how to thank God, and They won't tell me which of my beseechings and celestial bartering had actually sealed the deal. I promised much, of course. I would devote my life to good causes. I would gladly die in Their name. I would endure all the misery and gloom of a thousand desperate lifetimes if only They would keep my children happy and healthy, and I secured a book deal.

I fear, deep in my bones, that I've written a cheque that it will be damn difficult to cash. I'm horribly unhappy in my relationship but I'm taking this as some metaphysical penance: a payment in advance of some nominated reward. I'll take it all, I pledge. I'll do whatever you want. Just don't take this away.

A few weeks later I quit work. I'm not even having a particularly bad day. I've spent the past month writing the sequel to the first book, bashing it out entirely while sat at my desk and doing my damnedest to upset the bosses. Nobody notices, or if they do, my friends keep them away. And then I just say 'bugger this' and I walk. Somebody else sorts out the holiday pay and the official leaving day and nobody quite believes my friends when they explain that I've got a book deal and am leaving because I hate everybody else. But I don't go back. I never go back.

When the signature money comes in we go on holiday. Then another. We're in London a lot, having meetings. We sell the rights to America, Germany, Italy, Spain. We sell the TV rights. My publishers love the follow-up. The book is selected for the Richard and Judy Book Club and it's in the Sunday Times top ten. I'm interviewed on stage by my literary hero in front of 600 people, and I make everybody laugh with my irreverence and quips. The bookshop sells out of copies of the novel. They hadn't, they tell me, expected me to be so popular.

I wait for my depression to lift. I wait for the moment when I can lay down and feel good and look at myself and my life without revulsion. It doesn't come. I drink more, because it's free or I can afford it. I throw my money around because I want to get nice things for the people I like and love. I pay off debts and ask them to round the interest up to the nearest thousand as a gesture on my part. I book holidays and buy an extra dog. I pay for my mam and her new husband to go away on a holiday. I buy instruments for my stepson. Within a year we have four horses though none of us can ride. I still only feel something like contentment in the moments when I'm walking in the woods with Elora. My sense of peace only descends when I glimpse a barn owl in the morning light or one of the horses comes over to rub its head against mine while I drink a mug of tea and watch the sun go down. It's not meant to be like this. I'm back in therapy within a month of the book coming out. The comedown, the sense of anti-climax, is too much to stand. I run out of money. It's an age until the next book comes out. The planned tour of America doesn't materialize. My family adjusts to the idea of Daddy as a novelist and it's no longer anything to make people say 'wow'. And there's me, just me, same as ever.

The book sells well, of course. I'm on my arse financially on the day that I get the text message from the bank querying the large amount of money just deposited into my account. I rush to my desk and open my internet banking. I've just received £60,000 in Royalties. I step back, astounded, and step barefoot in a fresh dog shit. I'm laughing hysterically when they find me.

27

Self Portrait

My forehead's in my palm again. Back curved like a question mark.

We're prone to a hump, our family. Broad shoulders and baldness. Bad circulation, constipation, shiny shins.

Melancholia.

Rage.

Pit-pony legs jiggling up and down. Tip-toes beneath the desk. Looks like I'm limbering up for something - a sprinter limbering, loosening; fluid bones and heightened senses.

Hand on the mouse: a spider positioned to strike.

Bastard computer won't cooperate. Nothing and nothing then a something that's worse. Pages of nonsense. White on blue, like sea-spray and seagulls. Hieroglyphs and code.

Old, now. Slow. Past its prime. Too clogged up with old pictures, old files; books finished and unbegun. Kindred spirit, but I could smash its bastard face in when it doesn't play its part.

Adrenaline, now. Dopamine. Serotonin. Melancholia. Rage …

Words a zoetrope, spinning, spinning, desperate for release. Come on, come on, before it goes, before whatever it is that wants to be written finds another head to tunnel into …

Blue screen.

Black screen.

Look away. Fool the fucker. Don't touch it, you'll make it worse. That way. Look at something else. Anything. Down and to the left. Out the window and into the air. Weeds and gravel. Rabbit legs. An errant kidney. Ivar, guarding his spoils. The car and the wall and the sheep-skull and trees …

Grime on the lower sash. Thick: breath and fingerprints and coppery cityscapes. A Turin Shroud of matted cobweb at the top sash: a smear on greasy bifocals. Retreating, retreating, back through the glass.

Can't afford to pay the window cleaner. Nice lad. Does his best. Youngish. Doesn't whistle but looks like he has the potential. Seems quite taken with knowing a writer. Hasn't chased me up for the two missed payments yet. I give him a wee bit of banter on the doorstep when I'm telling him not to bother this time – linguistic currency, buying me another month. Make him laugh so he forgets the debt. I imagine a wife or girlfriend in charge of the accounts, twittering in his ear about the books not balancing. Hope that our little relationship somehow matters to him more.

Arrogant bastard. Believe your own rhetoric. Believe your own bullshit. Don't know if you really think this stuff or just say it for effect, but you are so obnoxious it makes people cringe ..

Down to the carpet. There's a space today. The books have drifted to the skirting boards. Toys spill out of repurposed boxes. Could do with running a vacuum over it. Could always do with running a vacuum over something. Dog hair. Cat hair. Sprinkled crisps and spilled juice brown doilies of boot-trod dirt.

Clicks. Whirs. A reminder ofr the importance of updating virus software. System unprotected. Exposed to hackers and viruses. What else is bloody new? Let the buggers clone me. Good luck to them. Go on, take the debts, you're welcome.

Blue screen.

Black screen.

When did we lose the egg-timer? The rainbow wheel? The little paperclip…

Awake now. Screensaver in monochrome. Elora, five or six, little shorts and sunglasses. Me, somnolent on a bench, shirt too tight, unbuttoned too far, staring up through shades and hat brim to give her my full attention. Drunk probably, looking back. Drunk and knackered and too hot. The Seine behind us. I half remember the day. I think she danced in the fountains outside the Louvre and some Japanese tourists took her picture. Oddly proud. I wonder whether Nicola would have approved. Somebody could have taken a fancy to her. Somebody could have nabbed her. She looked lovely though. Enjoyed it. Sparkled like the sun upon glass. Worth it, wasn't it? She must remember. Better call. Better check. No, she's at college. 17 in a couple of months. Not a *she*, neither. A *them*. A *they*. Try and keep up. This is your chance. You understand confusion. Contradiction. Subversion. You're snowflake and caveman, poet and thug. She needs your help through this. *They*, you prick…

Door opening. Nicola. Botticelli's Venus in grey pyjamas. Red toenails and Disney princess eyes. Good news! There was some money in the Etsy account. An instalment's gone in from the lady who bought the painting. Another from a client who'd put the transfer on hold. So that's good, isn't it/? Bad news. Sky payment's still to come out. Should have phoned them a year ago. Threatened to cancel and got a few months free as a sweetener. When's the rent? What about the council tax? The arrears or the new year's, I ask. Both. Either. Have we got something in place? What else is due in? Have you chased up that invoice? Sorry, I've disturbed you, I'll leave you to it.

Head in my palm again. The pain, just under the ribs and across the back. Another blood pressure test this morning; more needles jabbing in the crook of my arm, blood too turgid to flow.

A new document. Clean page.

Stick it on 200 per cent view. Times New Roman. 12pt. What kind of a monster can write in Calibri? Should do it automatically after ten years, truth be told. Should have the UK dictionary installed too. Should have worked out where the microphone is so I can teach my classes on something other than my bloody phone. State of the art, once. Best money could buy. Hour upon hour in PC World: guarantees, warranties, passwords and protections. We've got the Know-How, or some such bollocks. Wandered off, as far as I can recall. Me and Elora, gazing at tropical fish on bedspread TVs. Left stepmum to deal with it all. Stepmum to El, not to me. Don't know what she was to me, really. Jailer. Victim. Anchor-point. General manager. Good at this shit. Liked all that stuff – being in charge, being the boss, getting down to the nuts and bolts. Not my bag, baby. I was there to make them laugh: irreverent libertine; clever and naughty, elevated and worse. You have to meet this bloke, he's hysterical. Mind like a rocket, quick as a lash, haven't laughed this much in ages …

Couldn't sustain it. Bored now. Sick of myself. Bile at the back of my throat and fingers tingling for a drink. Came back when it was all over. Two grand plus. Celebrated by spending some money. Huge chap came to install it. Massive. Sweat dripping off him like butter. Thought he might have a heart attack on the stairs. Would have to flood the house to float him into the ambulance. Impressed to meet a writer. Always thought of writing a book but wouldn't know where to start. Salami fingers leaving their prints on ink black keys.

Little winking cursor. New document. Ctrl S. Call it '*Jottings*'. '*Me2*' has negative connotations and I don't want to jinx the thing with bad juju before I start.

Everything as it should be.

Clean, crisp, bone-white screen.

Not a thing to say.

28

A Whisky Business

Another night, another toilet cubicle. Elora is with me this time. She's eight or nine and she's listening to her Daddy cry. Daddy's been drinking for about four days straight but the drunkenness has only really taken hold in the last hour or so. I've been buying the drinks all night. This is our local, right in the middle of the square in the little market town in Lincolnshire. We live in the 'big white house on the hill'. Everybody knows us. They know I'm the writer. I've got my posters in tube stations and banners on the side of buses and my family is loud and friendly and different. Generous, too. I have a habit of secretly paying the dinner bill of people whose company I've enjoyed, or clearing the tab of some woe-begotten mate. I don't have the balls to announce that 'the drinks are on me', but they do tend to be a lot of the time. We eat here most nights. On the nights we eat at home, we come in for a drink either before or afterwords. They like us here. We're good, here. We make each other laugh and we can hold the attention of the crowd and we can't argue or shout at each other because it might spoil the illusion.

They know that we drink. Wine for her. Whisky for me. It's re-marked upon, but it's part of the character and it's frowned upon to be sanctimonious about alcohol consumption while sitting in a pub. Her son, my lad, meets us here after school most days. I arrive with Elora some time around 5. We're all so nice to each other, here. We all play our part.

It's hit me bad tonight. The drink helped, and then it didn't. I'm not in the mood for being social. People are irritating me. I'm tired but I don't want to sleep. I've been writing all day, but the sales from the second book are nothing like the sales from the first and my agent keeps telling me that it's important to have "realistic expectations" and to put some money aside "for a rainy day".

I'm feeling prickly. Angry, even. I'm feeling sorry for myself and sick of having to do everything myself. Nobody gets it. I don't really know what it is that they don't get, but their failings are winding me up. I'm not feeling any better about myself and I've had a genuine best seller. I was on the Richard and Judy list, for God's sake! I was on stage with Val McDermid being applauded by 600 crime fiction fans. Why isn't there some kind of pamphlet, counselling writers on what to do when the bubble bursts? Why aren't my publishers ringing to check that I'm feeling loved? Why am I so a pitiful, needy lugworm that I can't allow the good stuff that's happened to me to wash away all the bad that's come before?

I'm asking this through tears and snot and bile – my face against the cold wall. Elora is sitting on the closed lid of the toilet. She's seen tears in my eyes before but she's never seen me genuinely weep. I'm sobbing like a baby, my head on her knee as if she's the parent and I'm the child. She's so good at listening. She's the only one who says the right things. She's heard me say them to her, to other people, since she was tiny and I feel almost proud that she has the wherewithal to repeat them back to me. She throws some of her own in too. She tells me that I'm brilliant and the best Daddy ever and that my problem is I'm just not like other people and they're not like me, and that's why I can do amazing things when most people just settle for being pretty good or not dreadful. And she tells me that maybe I shouldn't drink quite so much, or maybe me and her stepmum might take it in turns to drink so that we don't do it at the same time and end up in a situation like tonight, where our private rows have become very public. She loves her stepmum, she tells me, but she's scary. She doesn't blame me for being frightened of her as well. It doesn't make me weak. Everybody's frightened of her, it's normal – she's scary. And she's got a stepbrother out of the situation, and that's worth everything else, and if we left we'd lose him, and I love him like he's my own, so it's worth it, on balance. Our life is good, she says, and that's because even before the book deal I always did whatever the hell I could to make sure we made more good memories than bad.

I'm holding a whisky in my fist. I've been sick a few times but it doesn't stop me drinking. I've paid for the damn stuff so I'm not going to waste it. I've had a tax bill. A VAT bill. Apparently we haven't paid the council tax and there's an old parking fine that now amounts to hundreds. My next chunk of money doesn't arrive for another three months. My partner is about to quit work to become my full-time manager, though I don't know if I need a manager or how I'll respond to one, and I only suggested it because I was sick of hearing about all the agonies she was enduring at work. Money solves everything, yeah?

I've told myself that most of my life. The gaps within me can be filled up with accomplishment; with cash; with hedonistic experiences. I don't want to amble and smell the flowers – I want to swagger, collar up, a cigarette in my smirk and rain on my sunglasses. I know who I am. I'm not this. Not this sniveling embarrassment who's scared of his girlfriend who doesn't even like this pub, or many of these people, and who would rather be at home reading a book and drinking tea and eating spaghetti on toast.

I tell her all this and she pretends she understands. She cuddles me. Tells me I'm brilliant again. Asks me if she wants me to go to the bar and get me another whisky. They let her get my drinks for me. They know her. She's Marko's daughter. I don't know if they think she's lucky or cursed.

I sort myself out, of course. I pull myself together. No point being Marko if you can't at least put the mask on and fool the masses. I tell her I'm sorry for being such a baby. Tell her that she's the best thing I've ever done and that she means more to me than any amount of literary success. She does, too. I'm capable of saying any amount of earnest bullshit but there are times when I mean it and everything I say to Elora is completely true. She was worth staying alive for. She means more to me than books. She's shown me what love looks like and feels like and I don't begrudge her the fact that she prevented me from killing myself. The fact I'm miserable isn't her fault. The fact that I'm ill isn't her fault. And she's the only one who makes me feel any better.

I'm sober now and a lot of the things I used to think and say and do feel as though they were the actions of another person. I feel shame. I feel true regret. I wish I'd done a lot of things differently. But I also know that the person I was and the person I am and the person I pretended to be are all different captains of the same ship and I've got better at passing the tiller to the one best suited for the particular job. And Elora seems relatively unscathed. She doesn't drink, which is hardly surprising. She hasn't spoken to her stepmother in five years and has only fleeting text chats with her stepbrother. Our little unit imploded when she was 12. By then we were broke and being chased by creditors and even a six figure book deal had only a fleeting impact on my spirits. We were always a good family unit on our holidays. Sun, sea, plenty of alcohol and good food, new experiences and nobody texting me suggesting I might like to slip away and come have some no-strings sex and feel briefly better about myself. In those circumstances, we were pretty awesome. It was reality we sucked at. I still suck at it, but at least now I'm a bit more sanguine about things and don't feel compelled to put on a show. 15 months without a sip of alcohol. I miss it. That doesn't seem quite enough, really. Imagine going the rest of your life without ever seeing your own reflection. That's how I feel about knowing I'll never drink again. But I'm a bit quieter. Calmer. Elora says I was more fun when I drank.

29.

Ha Ha Ha Ha. Staying Alive

He looks like a shrink. If I were to draw one, he'd look like this. Tall, slender, balding and kind-eyed. He's wearing a black polar neck beneath a rumpled blazer and his frameless glasses catch the light. He purses his lips as he listens but he doesn't hurry me. He lets me talk, even though I don't even know whether I'm making any sense. I'm not talking the way I usually do. I'm not scanning the conversation for potential jokes, or waving my hands, or asking questions. I'm flat. Numb. I'm speaking in a monotone, my face directed at the floor. This is our first session and I'm aware that an hour isn't very long to explain why I've been referred to the mental health team, or what it is I think and feel and want to put right.

I get depressed, I say. I am depressed. I see things that aren't there. I think about killing myself all the time but I can't kill myself because the kids need me, but maybe I'm just using that as an excuse and maybe they don't need me at all, but if that's the case then I've wasted years being alive and unhappy when I could have just gone and not caused any harm...

It's all gone wrong. I'm a few months away from throwing a hand grenade into our family unit. We're hanging on, just about. Me, Elora, her stepbrother and stepmum. He's off to university next year. The stepmum would like us to move to London but we can't because Elora still lives half the time with her real mum and that means we're geographically anchored. I'm facing a tax bill bigger than the amount of money I'm due in over the next 12 months. I haven't been invited abroad to see my foreign publishers in an age. My last couple of books have sunk without trace. I've got a new one coming out in a few months and everybody seems excited but I've been here before and I know that even if it becomes a massive hit, it won't really make a difference to what I'm feeling. We're living in a house I can't afford. We've got four bloody horses and none of us can ride. Elora's getting older and doesn't want to play with Daddy the way she did. She's arguing with her stepmum all the time. She's in her bedroom more and more. She's having anxiety attacks.

My head caved in a few weeks ago. I'd like to say that I'm talking figuratively but I'm not entirely sure. I felt it go. It was all just too much. Too many arguments, too little love, too much pressure and wishes and failures and drink. A friend of ours was staying with us, together with her two baby daughters. My stepson's friends were in and out of the house every five minutes. There was so much noise. I was having to be the person from the pub even when I was at home. There was never a moment when I could switch it off. My partner seemed to have forgotten it was all an act. I could keep it going forever as long as when we closed the bedroom door we lay down softly together and she stroked my head while I whispered against her tummy. But there was no gentleness in our relationship. No tenderness. Or maybe there was and I didn't notice it because I was drunk and so was she and I was trying to write a new book while providing for a rapidly expanding family and trying not to be caught out in any one of my lies.

The shrink listens for far longer than the hour. He's kind to me. He asks whether I plan to hurt myself and how far along those plans are. Tears come, but I don't sob, because that would require too much effort.

Yes, I say. I know the tree. It's a perfect tree.

I don't tell him that I imagine literary students of the future clamoring for a blue plaque to be erected there. I can imagine him going home and telling his wife that he's met the most grotesquely arrogant arsehole of his whole career.

Bi-polar 2, again. With hallucinations and an order of spicy fries. I need more talking therapy followed by focused Cognitive Behavioural Therapy. He's going to write to my GP and increase the dose of my anti-depressants. He's going to give me the number of the crisis team to call if I feel like I'm spinning out of control. Somebody will be in touch, he says, and he just wishes he were able to offer the therapy himself.

It won't be him. He's just the consultant. He makes the assessment and puts me on a list. It will be months before I get to start the programme. He wants me to know that I'm not alone and more people than ever are feeling like this.

Seven months later I get my appointment. I've put myself together to the best of my ability. I can pass for sane. I walk back into the same consulting room and there's a different chap sitting there. He asks me how I am and I tell him I'm okay, doing better, and he's delighted to hear it and makes a note on his computer and tells me he's pleased that the medication increase is working. He discharges me. I walk out in a daze, making a mental note to sound less positive in future when asked about my state of mind by a mental health professional.

A week later, I meet the love of my life. She's got colossal mental health problems and has spent 18 years trapped in a loveless marriage. Three kids, and no money, but she's gorgeous and she thinks I'm an amazing writer. I feel good about myself for the first time I can remember. I want us to be together but don't want to hurt anybody. And I'm scared that my partner might actually kill me. We'll have to take thing slowly, I say. You leave your husband, I'll leave her and then we can 'meet' properly in a few months when nobody's feeling swill be crushed beyond repair. She tells her husband about me the next day. I don't panic. I'm good in a crisis. And this is true love, after all. This is exciting. It's like being in a novel. The debts don't matter. My alcoholism doesn't matter. My depression makes me sexy, right? And her Borderline Personality Disorder and history of suicide attempts is proof of her passion and zest and artistic temperament. Our demons can play together.

She's pregnant five months later. And I'm broke. I'm also sober, and I feel good. I feel loved. I feel like I've found something that matters more to me than my ego and my misery and my desperate need to matter. I never want us to disentangle our arms and legs. I don't have nightmares any more. I don't want anybody else. It feels like all the love I've read about and written about all my life. I love listening to her and she listens when I talk. She doesn't shout at me and she thinks I'm clever and witty and kind. I spend three and a half grand on her engagement ring.

A year later, we sell it to pay off some of the debts. By now, she knows what I am. By now, we have a baby and four other kids between us and she's in the midst of a depression that puts mine to shame. And taking care of her means that I don't have to look at what's wrong with me.

I can keep this up for another 42 years. I've got this far, so I may as well crack on. And besides, I'm in love. Nicola, Elora, Artemisia, Nicola's kids. They give me purpose. They annoy the heck out of me most days but I like my life. I'm a depressive, but it stays in the shadows most of the time. Keeping busy keeps me sane. I feel able to look at aspects of myself without a drink in my hand. I give talks about mental health and I feel like I've kind of reached a place where I know who I actually am and am relatively okay with it. Nicola disagrees with me. She thinks I'm fragile and traumatized and that I will crack someday under the weight of all the pressures I heap on myself. But she's mentally ill.

I feel able to write about it all. To take little biopsies of my brain and splurge them onto a blank page to be examined by anybody with an interest in matters of the head. It's a bloody stupid idea and it stirs up all sorts of shit and makes me feel like I've never got well, and I've just had to phone the mental health charity to tell them that I'm not doing so well and need some kind of help, but on balance, and if it helps, I guess it's worth it.

Nicola tells me that she's proud of me, and that she loves me, but the finished product will "probably kill your mam". And Elora tells me she won't read it, because it will just be loads of me going on about myself and trying to work out whether I'm brilliant or awful, and she's listened to that for 17 years. Artemisia says she'll read it, but she can only recognise the letter A and thinks stories are rubbish unless they contain a dragon. Everyone's a critic.

30

Threesome, Foursome, Totally Awesome

"I think you need to put in some more stuff about the self-destructiveness. Fighting. Having sex with an affection-starved 63-year-old farmer's wife so she would persuade her husband to tow your car out of a ditch with his tractor. The sex and the drugs and the …"

"Rock and roll?"

"Sausage rolls would be funnier."

"I think it's been done."

"Who by?"

"Everyone. Literally everyone …,"

"Oh I'm sorry, excuse me if I don't have an encyclopedic knowledge of every single person who's used 'sausage roll' puns …,"

Nicola's lying in our bed and helping me decide what I think about stuff. I say this with great affection rather than malice. I often don't know what I think about stuff until I've talked to Nicola or written it down, or tacked together the yawning gaps in my perspective. It doesn't help that what I think about stuff depends entirely on my mood and my mood depends upon all manner of fluctuations and influences, both within and without. Hers too. The Venn diagram required to find the optimum moment for a heartfelt conversation looks very much like the Olympic logo, or the word "oooo.".

Even so, we talk a lot. We talk in the face of any actual evidence that it's good for either of us. When we're not talking about ourselves we're writing about ourselves or talking to other people about where we're at on our journey, which we are taking by ourselves, but together. We're both so horribly sensitive, insecure and belligerent that even deciding what to watch on TV this evening can descend into one or either of us thinking that the other is accusing us of having wasted our life and possessing all the intellectual sophistication of a pit-bull in jogging trousers.

It's taken us a long time to get on the same page in terms of morality, decency and how to live a life. There isn't just her and me in our relationship, there's all our hang-ups, insecurities and mental monsters too. She feels guilty a lot more than I do. I tend to bypass guilt and go straight to self-loathing. She looks back at her indiscretions with shame. I look back and think of them as part of the journey that led me to her, to here, to Artemisia and a career as a novelist. She wishes we had a monthly budget and remembered to write important things on the calendar and always brushed Artemisia's hair before school. I think we're Bohemian and a bit wrinkled around the edges and that society should forgive us our failings because we're creative types who can't be expected to deal with tedious, everyday shit. This is because I have low self-esteem and a monstrous ego and she, somewhat awkwardly, is somebody who remembers every conflicting thing that I say. It means that she doesn't know, for sure, whether I look back at my sexploits with pride, shame, or both. It's clear that when she's at her low points and the anti-depressants have robbed her of anything close to a sex drive, she's not exactly impressed about my past sexual escapades. But when she's feeling lively, she does squeal with glee at the sheer ridiculousness of some of the situations I've found myself in. It helps that I remember her primarily as the sweetly bookish mum-of-three who got in touch with me having read my second novel (set in the world of dogging and underground sex clubs) and who politely enquired who did my research as it was something she was keen to, ahem, know much more about.

"The book's about mental illness though," I say, sitting on the edge of the bed and feeling the rather pitiful flutter in my chest. "I don't know if writing about the criminal stuff and the messing around is anything to do with my mental health issues. What's shagging got to do with depression."

She literally laughs at me. She's good at this, is Nicola. She is a person who is literally incapable of disguising her state of mind and who believes that the phrase "but it's the truth!" is an adequate defence against unrestrainedly hurting somebody's feelings. When she's detected the scent of bullshit she can make her nostrils look like a shotgun.

"You slept with endless people because half the time you were frightened of hurting their feelings! You spent big chunks of your twenties couriering dodgy substances from one address to another and spending your time in pubs run by gangsters. You got into fights with people twice your size just to prove you weren't scared any more. What do you mean it's not about mental health?"

I don't have much in the way of a comeback when she gets all accurate about things. I sometimes regret being so damnably honest when we first got together. She found most of my stories quite sexy in our early days but she's got an astounding memory coupled with an innate pessimism so everything I've ever told her serves as inescapable proof that I'm a terrible person who will no doubt destroy her, her children and everything she holds dear before I'm through. I've never found it so difficult to argue with somebody as I do with Nicola. She's never where I think she's going to be in our dialogue and we're so rarely arguing about the thing I think we're arguing about. It's like turning up for a game of tennis and finding your opponent in armour, in horseback, and holding a lance. I know I'm articulate and I think I know what point I'm trying to make but after ten minutes in discussion with Nic I can feel my brain running out of my ears and double-knotting itself under my chin. She baffles me daily, and it often seems that what she said yesterday and what she's going to say tomorrow are continents apart, while being strongly held and equally valid viewpoints. But it keeps me on my toes.

"You look at me like I'm an arsehole a lot of the time," I say, pouting. "I realise that's because I'm an arsehole, but it still hurts. I've got that zappy feeling in my head. I feel all anxious. I hate it."

"How long have you been feeling like that?" she enquires, in that way of hers that makes me not notice the thin ice beneath my feet.

"A couple of days."

"So that's why I've been falling anxious! I've picked it up from you!"

This is a normal conversation in our house. Nicola is a lint-roller for other people's emotions. They invariably manifest in a countenance written in capital letters. Nicola's facial expressions are a recurring theme when we have disagreements. She often looks at me as if I'm an unanticipated pube in her Victoria sponge. And I don't have the bedrock of self-confidence that is required to feel anything other than upset in response. I don't have crutches to lean on any more. Or crotches, for that matter. Throughout my adult life I've had coping strategies that would be deemed "inadvisable" and "actions of a twat" by anybody with a whiff of decency about them. But which are also, bizarrely, indicators of being, in some circle, a bit, well, cool.

I'll explain. When I get upset, I don't like it. When I feel picked upon, I don't like it. When I feel like I've failed, it eats away at me. So I need to make myself feel better. I have to prove to myself that I'm not feeble, not weak, not a big girl's blouse. And for 20 years, that has meant doing something that most other people couldn't' do, or wouldn't do. It has meant starting fights with people bigger than me. It's meant seducing the wives and girlfriends of the loudmouths who cut me off mid-sentence or who've made fun of my height or lack of hair. It's meant agreeing to go pick up money from somebody who might not want to hand it over. It's meant responding to one of the women, or men, who've texted me something suggestive, and agreeing to meet up for intense, cinematic sex somewhere that we could easily be caught. It's meant trying new drugs and old drugs and mixed drugs. It's meant wading in to pub fights have nothing to do with me. It's meant sex clubs and sex saunas, sex cinemas and an endless procession of assignations with the bored, the disaffected, the lovelorn and the intensely horny.

Have I ever met up with somebody out of straightforward sexual desire? Not really, no. I've got self control. I wouldn't risk everything just to get my rocks off. But to prove to myself that I'm not a pitiful nobody? To get my own back, on some level, against the people who've overlooked me or not see my potential? Yeah, for that, I'd risk it all. And when you live like that, with your radar constantly picking up signals, you find that there are an awful lot of people looking for something outside of their relationship. They're often looking for the same thing as you. Sometimes they get a little obsessive and it becomes a Herculean task to extricate yourself from the 'relationship' without hurting their feelings. In such cases, my innate cowardice has meant that I've kept seeing them, desperately hoping that they will see the truth beneath the lie and put me out of my misery with a final goodbye.

"I understand why you might not want to write about this stuff," she says. "It's going to be hard for people to like you when they read about all the arsehole stuff you used to do. If I'd known the full story I'd have run a mile."

She always makes me question stuff, does Nicola. I like to give answers, not just responses. So I think about it properly and wonder whether it matters to me whether people 'like' me or not, and whether that judgement can be formed on the basis that I used to be into some shady stuff and had a habit of falling into people's wives.

"I don't think I care," I decide. "Look who my heroes are. Pablo Neruda, Charles Bukowski, Lord Byron – all mad shaggers with the morals of an alley cat. But they're literary colossus so it's kind of priced in. Maybe that's why I was always so excited to become something of note, as it would kind of legitimatize my cuntishness."

I look at her hopefully, optimistic that my self-knowledge and poetic profundity will persuade her that my sins should be overlooked and that she should probably, on balance, take her clothes off. She laughs at me again. I leave in a sulk.

I don't really know how to go about telling you the ins and outs and the shake-it-all-abouts of my sexual gallivanting. I don't really think it's relevant, or if it is, there's probably another book in it and I should keep my powder dry. I won't say that it ever had the desired effect of making me feel marvelous, but I did always get a distinct buzz from the seduction and the secrets and the sense that I was living in the movie version of my own life. I can't say I felt especially guilty, even when already ensconced in serious relationships. And yeah, now that I behave myself and am fully in love, I fully realise what an absolute bell-end that made me. All I can say in my defence was that I felt as though choosing not to die was already a grand enough gesture. Putting other people first meant that I was a decent partner. Seeing other people on the side was almost recreational. I treated it like some people treat golf. And now I've got this far I may as well tell you that I have always found it massively easier to embark upon a sexual encounter with a stranger than it is to go through the complex negotiating tactics necessary to make love to one's own long-term partner. And yes, I know, what little sympathy you had for me before has now evaporated and as far as you're concerned I'm a beast and a monster and worse, a man. But that doesn't really have much of an impact on somebody who was trying to drink themselves to death and who kept putting themselves in dangerous situations so that their death wouldn't be officially suicide.

Anyway, that was all the past. I'm older and less of a shit and I know for a fact that Nicola would literally cut my balls off and staple them to my forehead if I even looked twice at the flirty lady in the fruit shop, so it's not really worth the risk. And Nicola can make me feel better about myself with a kiss or a kind word than I used to feel post-threesome, foursome or totally-awesome.

But there you go. I've hidden nothing. You can't say I haven't been totally honest. But there'll be more in book two.

31.

Continuing to Not Die

It goes wrong for years. Each book sells less well. We lose the foreign deals. The TV adaptation doesn't come off. I get into extraordinary levels of tax debt. I'm in and out of therapy and my partner and I are drinking so much that there isn't really a time of day between hangover lifting and the first sip of whisky or wine. I'm a better writer than ever and my personality fits into the world like a hand into a silken glove, but somehow, it's all wrong. All my fault. All the result of me being such a wretched, wretched loser.

Somehow, after a few years as a novelist, I've spent more than I've ever earned, and have double that amount in debt. I still don't quite know how I did it.

And then my agent rings. A bigger publishing house wants to reignite my career. They think I'm brilliant. They're offering 300,000 for a three book deal.

And I know that the misery has indeed been a payment. I know that I'm being given another chance, and all I have to do is endure the life I've been given, and stay in a relationship so devoid of affection and tenderness that I feel as though I must be made of spikes and slime.

I waste the money, of course. And the books continue to flop. And by then I don't care about the consequences of breaking my deal with the universe. By then, I'm in such mental purgatory that all I want is a way out.

When it comes, it's 5ft 6" and breathtakingly beautiful. It's love at first sight for the pair of us. I'd give up my book career for her in an instant. I'd do anything just to feel her cheek against mine; her heart pressed to my own; beating in tandem with a soul that feels like a mirror for my own.

A few months later, I experience a moment of true bliss. We're at the most northerly point in Iceland in deepest December; the sun barely rising and the landscape a great frieze of sparkling black and jagged white. I'm with the love of my life. She truly is my everything. We've had to hurt people to be together but for once, everything feels as though it was meant to be and something this marvelous can't possibly be wrong. My daughter adores her and I get on with her kids and promise them life is about to be much more interesting.

We start 2017 on a high. I'm sober. And she's pregnant. And everything feels inconceivably wonderful. Depression? Drink? Suicide? I can't even remember the urge.

When she arrives, we call her Artemisia. She's amazing. We decide to move to the countryside for a fresh start. Elora, now 12, doesn't want to leave her friends but by the time she tells me this we've already found a house and started planning the move. Nicola's son, too, decides to stay with his dad.

It turns out we're as fragile as ever. We both spiral into the darkness. We have a baby now. A baby that doesn't care about our illnesses. A baby that needs one of us, or both. The post-natal depression is half killing my partner. She's so wracked with guilt and self-loathing that she convinces herself that all the things going wrong in our life are because of the people we've hurt and the things we've done wrong. She tells me I'm a terrible person. Tells me I'm the devil. Tells me she wishes we'd never met and that I lied when I told her I was a sure thing and that my books were definitely going to start selling in greater number. She can't believe she's had a child with me.

We get her the help she needs. We can't afford it and she'd really rather I let her kill herself the way she wants to, but I know she can beat this. It takes time. Takes great pain. I break my hand in three places punching a wall when she tells me I'm not strong enough to deal with her misery and my own.

But I stay off the booze. I take whatever paying gig I can find and I write more, better books than I ever have before. I take pleasure in my family and the animals and all the things that a person does when they have no money. I fall deeper in love with my partner every day. When she emerges from the darkness, there's a bond between us stronger than anything I ever imagined could exist outside of the pages of a book.

For the first time, I'm a Depressive who's not excessively Depressed. I'm an alcoholic who doesn't need a drink. I've got no rituals or routines save telling the people I love that I love them, and drinking at least eight cups of tea a day. I feel dangerously close to content.

It seems the perfect time to write a memoir about my years of utter, devastating unhappiness. After all, who wouldn't want to dive back in to that particular swamp?

I doubt it's inspirational, but it's helped me, in a way. I hope it does the same for you.

Well done, for being alive. I know it's a damn sight harder than the alternative.

THE END

ACKNOWLEDGEMENTS

Where to bloody start? Loads of people have helped keep me alive over the years. Some are still part of my life, some are long gone, or hate me, or both. So I'll just give a manly nod in the general direction of those who have helped turn these thoughts and feelings and memories into something approximating a book.

So, in no order whatsoever, if you're on this list, you have my gratitude. If you're not on the list and think you probably should be, it's because I'm a bit shit. (There's a longer list of people who did bugger all to help, but my therapy dictates that I don't allow my resentment to fester, so I'll send them a little silent kiss instead).

So, big love to: Linda Nagle, Mike Gower, Sarah Morgan, Brian Price, Domenica De Rosa, Luke Wood, Di Gammage, Rasheeda Azam, Roz Watkins, Linda Lee-Page, Nadia Mallin, Catherine Hunter, Matthew Sweet, S J Watson, Sarah Stovell, Susi Holliday, Ann Cleeves, Bryan Dick, Rebecca J Bradley, Neil Lancaster, Steve Dunne, Mary Picken, Linda Wright, Anne Cater, Donna Morfett, Roger Lytollis, Richard Vergette, Caroline Maston, Samantha Brownley, Claire Birkin, Chris Bennett, Tony Blake, Burnsy, Gill Holloway, Adrian Searle, Barbara Copperthwaite, Paddy Magrane, Mike and Jo Craven, Sandra Pedrick, Richard and Tracey O'Connor, Lisa Baxter, Derek Farrell, Gill Hart, Rita Lawson….

I'll stop. It's not the fucking Oscars.

Special mention, however, to my family, for permitting all this, and cooperating, and keeping me going time and again. Mam, Dad, Bernard, Phil, Selina, I love the lot of you. Elora Cordelia, or whatever you're calling yourself today, you remain the thought that calms my nerves and makes me smile. Artemisia, I'm so grateful for you, you mad little squirrel. Amber, Honey, Connor, I'm glad to have you in my life. Try and eat less sugar. Rachel the Witch, you've been a spellbinding amigo this past couple of years. Sarah, as ex-wives go, you're one of the best. Steve P, you're always there for me and it hasn't gone unnoticed. You're my own guardian angel. Ronni and Richard – you're odd, but marvelous. Dr Brian Lavery, of course. You're an unusual choice for a role model, but it's seen me right so far. You're a genuine pal.

And Nicola. My love. My reason and my madness, my earth and Heavens; my unfathomable darkness and immaculate light. You are my hero, my best friend, my perennial source of abject bewilderment and the most talented person I've ever met. I love loving you. Thank you.

David Mark, September 2021

Printed in Great Britain
by Amazon